TRAILS OF AN
ALASKA GAME
WARDEN

TRAILS OF AN ALASKA GAME WARDEN

Ray Tremblay

ALASKA NORTHWEST PUBLISHING COMPANY
Anchorage, Alaska

MT

Library of Congress cataloging in publication data:
Tremblay, Ray, 1926-
    Trails of an Alaska game warden.
    1.Tremblay, Ray, 1926-   2. Game wardens—
Alaska—Biography.   I. Title.
SK354.T74A38   1985   363.2'8   85-11174
ISBN 0-88240-304-4

Design by Pamela S. Ernst
Photographs by Ray Tremblay
Drawings of wilderness scenes by Sig Olson

Alaska Northwest Publishing Company
Box 4-EEE, Anchorage, Alaska 99509

Printed in U.S.A.

8/13/86

This book is dedicated
in memory of my son
Ron

Contents

Foreword

THOSE OF US WHO WORKED beside Ray Tremblay in managing and protecting Alaska's fish and game in "the good old days" of the 1950s and 1960s, know the mark he made. Alaska's wildlife professionals have long been close-knit: The handful of men who in those years worked for territory, state, and federal governments knew one another intimately. Among these dedicated men, Ray Tremblay stood out. To his co-workers no higher praise could be given than to say, "He always put the resource first," — which Ray did.

Not only did he put the resource first, Ray Tremblay was a leader and an innovator whose tireless efforts went far beyond the requirements of his law enforcement assignments.

My knowledge of Tremblay's professional career comes from firsthand observation. We met in 1953 when I was at Minto Lakes, near Fairbanks, banding waterfowl for the U.S. Fish and Wildlife Service, a summer break from my job of teaching wildlife management at the University of Alaska. Ray Tremblay arrived to fly me home to Fairbanks in a Piper Pacer.

From that first meeting sprang a friendship that has lasted more than three decades. We are tied together by a mutual interest in Alaska's fish and game. We have crossed trails in Alaska's wild places from the arctic Brooks Range to the Alaska Peninsula. We have attended the same wildlife meetings. Some of my former wildlife students worked for and with Ray. We have mutual friends who are mostly wildlife professionals or old-time Alaskans who have known the far places.

Ray Tremblay has plunged at life with enthusiasm, which the reader will perceive bubbling over on every page of this,

his second book recounting his adventures in Alaska. He takes an interest in everything and everyone around him. He has always been genuinely concerned over the well-being of others.

In this book Ray briefly recounts the rescue of a prospector at Big River, near McGrath. His modest account needs expanding:

It was June 1959, and U.S. Game Management Agent Raymond H. Tremblay was on an aerial search for the lost prospector. After much flying he sighted the man waving at him from a sandbar of Big River, which flows into the Kuskokwim River not far from McGrath.

The river was winding and narrow, with bank erosion and sweepers — fallen trees hanging from the shores. The current was swift and the water muddy.

Ten times Ray flew low-and-slow over the stranded man, searching for a spot to land. He studied the roily water, memorized where the sweepers were, and tried to judge the water depth.

He finally flew *below* overhanging trees, keeping the plane centered over the deeper fast water, and landed on a pinpoint he had located during his flyovers. He ran one float of the plane up on the river bar where the man stood, and held it there with power. While Ray kept the plane in position, the man plunged into the water, climbed up on a float, and crawled into the plane.

With the prospector aboard, Ray roared down the narrow river, dodging sweepers and shallow water, seeking a straight place where he could lift into the air without hitting bank-side trees.

In this perilous manner he sped around three bends until he found a relatively straight stretch. Firewalling the throttle, he lifted into the air and flew over the riverbank trees.

Fred A. Seaton, Secretary of the Interior, conferred the Valor Award of the Department of the Interior upon Ray for this feat. He commented, "By foresight, follow-up, and skillful execution, without regard for his personal safety, Mr. Tremblay undoubtedly saved the life of a fellow citizen."

Another Secretary of the Interior also found reason to bestow an award upon Ray Tremblay. In December 1979, Secretary Cecil Andrus awarded him the Interior Department's Meritorious Service Award for a highly superior performance and devotion to duty — recognition for his years with the U.S. Fish and Wildlife Service.

Andrus commented on Ray's sincere concern for the

well-being and wise use of the fish and wildlife in Alaska, his efforts in adapting aircraft to accomplish U.S. Fish and Wildlife Service missions in Alaska.

Those of us who have known and worked with Ray for the past three decades or more, also know the measure of the man: awards are nice, but we know that Ray's real reward has always been his personal satisfaction for simply doing his job to the best of his ability.

As Ray has written in this modest volume describing some of his conservation work, the 1950s were truly "the good old days" when Alaska was wild and free, without today's acrimony and clutter of laws involving use of fish and game. These lively tales recounting his adventures as an Alaska game warden (his titles were different, but that's what he was), based on his diaries, bring back fond memories for those of us who were there, and they will entertain, inform, and excite those who weren't.

Jim Rearden, Outdoors Editor
ALASKA® magazine

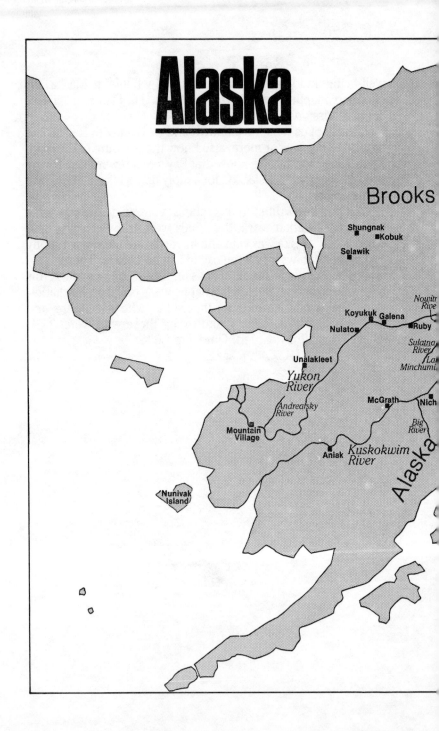

Alaska

Brooks

Shungnak
■Kobuk
Selawik

Nowitn
Rive
Koyukuk Galena
Nulato■ ■Ruby
Sulatna
River
La
Minchumi

Unalakleet

*Yukon
River*

*Andreafsky
River*

McGrath Nich

Mountain
Village

Big
River

Aniak *Kuskokwim
River*

Nunivak
Island

Alaska

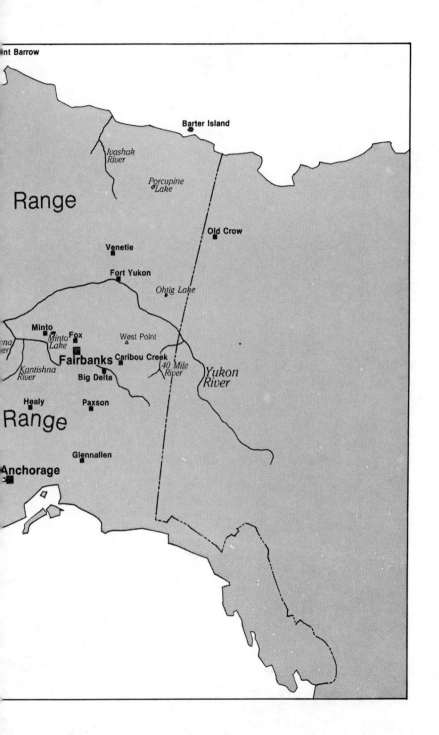

The Making of a Game Warden

I was a full time professional trapper in interior Alaska, a life I had dreamed of as a boy. Trapping for a living required a lot more work than I had envisioned, and it sometimes became very lonely. Not exactly the romantic life I had envisioned. Nevertheless it suited me. I loved the wilderness and the independent life, as well as the challenge of wresting a living from the land. I felt I was in control of my life. (I told a bit about my life as a trapper in *Trails of an Alaska Trapper,* published in 1983 by Alaska Northwest Publishing Company.)

But there were forces over which I had no control. In the spring of 1952, a scant three years after I took to the trapline trails, fur prices dropped to an all-time low. As I took my winter's catch of marten, mink, otter, and wolves to Fairbanks fur buyers to bid on, I became downhearted with the scant monetary reward for a hard winter of work.

I remember caressing the lovely dark pile of 122 marten skins as they lie on the counter of the highest bidder and my being bitterly reluctant to part with them for the paltry average of $27 a pelt. The buyer was sympathetic, but he could afford to be.

"I'm giving you a break, Ray," he said. "Since I know you've pulled the matched sets from this bunch, and I'm not getting the benefit of your best skins."

I thought of the nine silky furs I had left in my room at the Nordale Hotel, wondering if they would bring enough to offset the low price I was receiving for the rest of the catch. Holding out matched skins was common practice among trappers, especially those in the Minchumina area where I trapped, and

1

the upper Kuskokwim country, where marten vary from a light buff to chocolate brown. Some were even orange or light yellow and were humorously known as "Minchumina canaries".

I had sorted my catch in strong light and pulled out the matching skins or "blenders"as they were called. Out of 100 skins I would usually get about four sets of perfectly matched furs. Most marten chokers were made in sets of three skins. These, then, brought a premium price and I usually sold them by advertising in the *Fairbanks Daily News Miner* or by word of mouth around town. They brought $225 to $250 a set, depending on whether they were female or male pelts, the males bringing more because of their greater size

It took about six weeks before I got my price for the matched sets. Meanwhile I had brought my outfit, including the sled dogs, to Fairbanks for the summer. With fur prices so low I had to think about the future. Grub and other supply prices were rising, and fur prices were dropping, leaving me little choice.

I started working on my commercial pilot's license, working at odd jobs to pay the cost. At mid-summer all my dogs, boarded at a private kennel, contracted distemper and died. This seemed to be the final blow.

Pilot training progressed nicely, and I felt I had the necessary talents to qualify as a bush pilot. A big obstacle was finding an air taxi operator who was willing to take on an enthusiastic young pilot with a new, dripping-wet license and no practical experience. At that time much of the bush flying called for landings and takeoffs where airstrips didn't exist. Instead sandbars were used, or short, usually rough landing strips were hacked out by trappers, miners, and other back country dwellers. I was familiar with that part of the operation, having prepared a few strips myself at remote cabins.

As I explained my qualifications to one local air taxi operator he smiled and said, "After you've busted up a few planes flying the boonies, come back and we'll talk about a job."

Catch 22. In other words, go practice with someone else's airplanes. I would have to learn to maneuver aircraft in places manufacturers never dreamed their planes would operate before I could qualify to fly an operator's equipment. The problems were how to find who had planes that were expendable, and how do you bust airplanes without hurting yourself?

No one at Fairbanks could help me. It became obvious I

would have to look at other ways of achieving this goal. A thought occurred one day while I was talking with another trapper about the increased number of wolves around the country and the detrimental effect they were having on caribou and moose. Why not be a government trapper? I became acquainted with Frank Glaser, dean of wolf trappers for the U.S. Fish and Wildlife Service, and from his stories of the wolf-control program, my trapping experience and flying knowledge seemed made to order for a career in his field. At the time, aerial hunting of wolves with a shotgun was becoming a common method of control used by the federal government. I submitted my application, but, unfortunately, no position was available.

The seed was sown, however, and I started to beat a steady trail to the U.S. Fish and Wildlife office in Fairbanks. I became acquainted with the enforcement division of the service, and one day the secretary casually suggested that I might consider working as a game warden. This caused a new set of mental gears to mesh, and I mulled it over for some weeks.

I had to answer several questions for myself. Would I be able to enforce conservation laws, which I fully believed in, impartially, and with feeling for the people as well as the wildlife? Would I be able to live the life of a civil servant under the regimentation required of a government employee after living the free life of a woodsman? These and other questions plagued me for the next few months until one day fate struck again. A position became open for an enforcement agent pilot trainee: Would I accept it?

The pros and cons bedeviled me. Fur prices were down and the outlook was bleak. Why not give it a try? Here was a chance to put my skills to work at something worthwhile. I knew the subsistence way of life, as well as recreational hunting and fishing: Both are valid, and both have a substantial impact of Alaska's wildlife. I had a good knowledge of poachers' tricks, not because I had used them, but because they were often discussed by trappers and hunters with whom I associated. My piloting ability was progressing nicely, although I hadn't busted any airplanes yet. I thought of the old adage, "If you can't whip 'em, join 'em." So join them I did. I spent a quarter of a century protecting wildlife.

At first I was called an Alaska wildlife enforcement agent. This title changed in 1956 to U.S. game management agent, to conform with the title given federal agents in the Lower 48 states.

By the early 1970s important new laws protected diminishing wildlife. The illegal taking of wildlife was big business the world over, and congress enacted legislation to protect rare, threatened, and endangered wildlife. There are always those few persons who are willing to take a species down to the last animal for the monetary reward, giving us an ever-growing list of extinct animals. Our agents tackled international smuggling rings that shipped endangered mammals, birds, and reptiles in and out of the U.S. Domestic wildlife was being harvested in large numbers in violation of state and federal laws, and it became obvious that our investigative techniques needed to become more sophisticated. We then trained in the same academies as other federal law enforcement agencies. My title changed again, this time to special agent (wildlife), to more properly identify the work I was doing.

This progressive change of duties took me more and more out of the field and into the office. I was given more administrative responsibility and in consequence, more advancement, until I finally reached the position of chief of the Enforcement Division in Alaska for the U.S. Fish and Wildlife Service.

I have never regretted my choice of career. After 25 years of service (which ended in 1978) I could look people in the eye and say I gave it my best. I did my best to be fair in all decisions which affected many lives during my quarter of a century of service.

This then is the story of my life as a game warden in Alaska. The first six years were the most rewarding and interesting and are the basis for most of the chapters. Alaska was still a territory during those six years, and Alaska's Natives were still largely living from hunting and fishing, although the transition to today's mixed and mixed-up lifestyle had started.

Dog teams and snowshoes were the main mode of travel for those living on traplines, since snow machines had not yet made their debut. Liquor was a problem, but not an epidemic, as it is today. Drugs were unheard of in rural Alaska. The people were basically honest, resourceful, and they had a sense of pride in their way of life. Although Alaska wildlife enforcement agents never won any popularity contests, those who lived by the old standards understood the need for conservation laws, and they respected our work.

Recreational hunters were just beginning to flex their muscles. All terrain vehicles had not yet been developed (except in the form of the expensive military surplus tracked weasel), so these Nimrods were confined to local areas accessible only to the few highways that then existed. Small planes were taking hunters and fishermen into the back country, but they were not yet numerous enough to cause serious problems. Unscrupulous guides hadn't yet developed their devastating skills at driving bears and other wildlife with Supercub airplanes to the big money client, who, unable to walk, was stationed at a strategic location. Here he waited with a high-powered rifle for the exhausted and bewildered quarry to show up in a clearing to meet an undignified death.

Many of the old-timers were still around to tell stories of the "good old days," and they commonly started their hunting tales by saying, "Remember now, this happened before there were any game laws." Interestingly, the time frame they were talking about was 35 to 40 years prior to my early years as a warden, which is about the same number of years as between then and now.

A resident fishing license was $1; resident hunting and fishing $2; and resident trapping, hunting, and fishing, $3. There were only 6 game and fur districts (today there are 26 major ones, with numerous subdistricts), and the hunting, fishing, and trapping regulations were simple and easy to understand.

How times have changed. I remember conducting the annual game hearing at Fairbanks at the Tanana Valley Sportsman's log building on the bank of the Chena River. The meeting was open to the public, and it was the time for hunters and fishermen to request changes in the regulations — and/or to vent their frustrations on the U.S. Fish and Wildlife Service. The meeting lasted until after midnight, which I felt was much too long. Little did I realize how short a meeting it was by today's standards.

Nowdays the boards of fisheries and game are annually in session for several weeks to consider changes recommended by the Department of Fish and Game, advisory committees, regional councils, sportsmen's groups, and the public. Boards commonly are in session 14 hours a day listening to testimony and making decisions based upon recommendations of wildlife experts, professional biologists, attorneys, and the interested layman.

The state is cut up into so many districts and subdistricts

that it is difficult to locate some of the boundaries. Some regulations are so complex that state Fish and Wildlife Protection Officers cannot agree among themselves on how to interpret the intent, and, consequently, they have difficulty in enforcing the regulations. The same holds true for prosecuting attorneys and courts. Imagine the plight of the poor hunter confronted with the maze of regulations whenever he plans a simple hunt. I know several ex-hunters who have hanged up their rifles rather than take a chance on being prosecuted for an unintentional mistake.

In retrospect, it seems that life was infinitely simpler in the 1950s, and now that period is regarded by many Alaskans as the "good old days." Wolf hunter Frank Glaser, now hunting wolves in a happier land, and that dean of the old-time guides, the late M.W. "Slim" Moore, would, if they were here, argue that the "good old days" were the 1920s and the 1930s. Most of the real old timers who are now gone would probably call the time around the turn of the century the "good old days." Whatever the time span claimed as best, it had its good features, but there is no denying the truth that because of increasing human pressures, wildlife management becomes more complicated with each passing year.

It seems fitting to me that an account of the 1950s should be documented from at least the perspective of one warden of the time. Perhaps in years to come this account can be used to measure the progress of civilization and its confict with wildlife.

Chapter 1

District Patrols

I RECEIVED AN ANONYMOUS letter at my McGrath office one February, telling me about three moose that had been killed during closed season by villagers at Pilot Station, a small village on the bank of the Yukon River. "Get there right away while the evidence is still available,"the letter writer advised.

I flew the 250 miles to the village in a ski-equipped FWS (Fish and Wildlife Service) plane and was met by several village elders who wanted to know the purpose of my visit.

"I want to discuss the illegal killing of moose that I have heard about," I told them.

"Will you stay the night and meet with the men of the village?" they wanted to know.

Of course I would, and I was given a place to stay, after which I secured the plane for the night. My gear, including the oil drained from the engine of the plane, was moved to my assigned cabin by a couple of young boys pulling a small dog sled.

When there was a problem involving an entire Native village a meeting was held in the largest building of the community. Often this was the school, a meeting house, or, occasionally, the village bath house. These bath houses were built of log and covered with dirt, and were at least 20 by 20 feet. There was a low tunnel entrance usually covered by a bear skin and you stepped down onto a pole floor. A fire pit about 6 feet by 6 feet was in the middle. It contained large rocks, and had a smoke vent directly over-head. A single bench was built around the perimeter of the log walls. A village bath usually preceded community meetings. A large fire was built in the pit in order to heat the rocks. When all was ready the naked men all filed in and poured water on the rocks and sat in the steam-filled room discussing village problems, hunting, trapping, or whatever the current topic might be. After the men finished the women took over, and I assume they discussed their own particular problems. Later, when everyone had finished with their steam baths, the meeting would be held.

I was not invited to join in the sweat bath that night, but was sent for after the men had finished the ritual. Crawling through the tunnel I went from -40 degrees F. outside temperature to a steamy 120 degrees F. inside. This required the immediate shedding of clothes down to T-shirt. The chief of the village introduced me and acted as interpreter, which was customary in most villages since the majority of the older people spoke little or no English.

I felt it necessary to explain the job of the FWS and the reasons for game regulations because a meeting of this kind had never been held in the village, according to the chief. I also explained that we were very concerned with the moose population, for moose were just beginning to extend their range to the region. Moose were only occasionally found this far west, but due to a healthy build-up of the Interior populations, the animals were beginning to show up on the tundra in increasing numbers. A few had been seen along the Bering Sea.

How do you explain population dynamics and game management principles through a translator to a meat-hungry people who depend on hunting to live? Whenever one of these villagers found a moose track, it was followed until the moose was killed, no matter the distance or the hours and days it required. The tenacity of these hunters is recorded in my field diary of December 1956. "One Native at Tuluksak, who is partially blind but is considered one of the best hunters in the village, earned his moose the hard way during the second season. He traveled up the Tuluksak River with his dog team until he crossed fresh moose tracks. He then tied up his dogs and took off on foot following the tracks. Twenty-three and one-half hours later he got close enough to kill the moose, a young bull. After butchering the animal he went back for his team and hauled the meat 35 miles back to the village. All of this in temperatures of 25 degrees below zero."

After I had explained the reasons for protecting the growing moose population and the need for their cooperation, I tackled the problem at hand — the three illegal moose. A lengthy discussion ensued and the chief explained that there was little food in the village due to a poor fishing season. Any game taken, whether it be ptarmigan, grouse, rabbits, or in this case, moose, is divided among all the families, with the older people and families with children receiving the biggest pieces.

When the talks were finished I was taken on a tour of every home and what was left of the meat was displayed in pots and pans on stoves or in the entryways of the cabins. Each family had received about 20 pounds of meat, and every bit of the moose was consumed, including the intestines. Here was a true example of people living off the land and having to endure a difficult winter because of a failure of their main crop — the salmon run. There was some welfare in the village, which was also shared, but not enough to cover basic food needs. I gleaned this information next day from the school teacher and the Catholic mission at St. Mary's located down river from Pilot Station.

It was decision time for me, so the next night another meeting was set up in the bath house. We discussed the moose population problem again, and the consequences of killing off the animals before they were able to establish themselves in this area. I also lectured them on the laws, how they were formulated, the purpose they serve, and the consequences of violations. They listened intently as the chief translated back to the Native tongue. I told them I would not take any legal action on the three moose, but that in the future I expected that they would consider the implication of killing off a population of animals that would be of great benefit to them and their children in future years. They thanked me, said they would cooperate, and hoped they would be able to supplement their food supplies with small game and the fur animals they trapped so they wouldn't have to break the law again. I departed on this note, feeling I had accomplished my mission, vowing to continue these meetings in all the remote villages.

Upon my return to McGrath I found two local trappers awaiting me. They had quarreled over the ownership of beaver houses and wanted me to mediate. After listening to both I advised them that neither of them could claim exclusive trapping rights to any beaver houses regardless of how many years they had trapped the area.

They trapped on the north fork of the Kuskokwim River,

about two days by dog team from McGrath. They had already lost more than a week of trapping, and I suggested that since they were the only two trappers in their part of the country, they split the houses 50-50 and go back trapping. They accepted my solution (one they should have reached by themselves) and left the next day to continue trapping. What started out to be a blood feud with each trapper threatening bodily harm to the other ended amiably with each getting his limit of 10 beaver.

Another patrol finished and I was now faced with the paper work. Reports and more reports: I often wondered where they ended. Today I find that many are the basis for ongoing wildlife studies providing insight into an era that is gone, one that can never return, for like it or not, the twentieth century has arrived in bush Alaska.

A district that encompasses thousands of square miles and receives heavy resource use requires year-round patrols by a game warden. Being a realist he knows that he will apprehend but a small percentage of those who commit game violations. However, he also knows that if he can get the respect of the people they will help him protect the wildlife that is so vital to their welfare. As people almost entirely dependent upon fish and game for their livelihood, most were aware that without the wildlife agent, game warden, fur warden, bush cop, fish cop, or whatever his designation in the particular part of Alaska he worked, fish and wildlife numbers would rapidly diminish.

Taking an extra moose from a small herd, a few extra beaver from a limited watershed, or an extra net full of fish from a spawning stream will not in itself significantly impact the populations. But one successful poacher is enough to encourage a multitude of others to share the game, and that's when wildlife gets into trouble. Couple such indiscriminate taking with one or two severe winters that take their tolls on wildlife, and serious problems develop.

History has documented the demise of the buffalo, the passenger pigeon, and other targets of man's greed. With the blueprint of history to learn from, such decimation shouldn't be repeated, but to believe this is to position yourself with the ostrich whose head is in the sand. Left to his own devices, man will reduce wildlife to the last mammal, bird, or fish to satisfy his own needs, be they monetary, personal gain, ego, or a misguided idea of ethnic "right."

The only effective management tool to hold wildlife stocks in balance is the enforcement of sound laws and regulations. In order to accomplish this the warden must gain the respect of the public and the judicial system responsible for determining the guilt or innocence of those accused. An added burden was placed on those of us who were wardens in outlying areas of Alaska during territorial days because we initiated complaints before U.S. commissioners, acted as the prosecuting attorney, and made recommendations on penalties.

U.S. commissioners in bush Alaska were appointed by federal judges, and many selections were not based on competency: the problem was to find a village resident willing to accept the position. It was often necessary to instruct a new commissioner on how to conduct an arraignment, and to assure that the accused understood his right to a trial. The job didn't pay much, and commissioners were not afforded any special offices or equipment except for a safe in which to keep documents. Arraignments, coroner's inquests and trials were held in the commissioners' homes, which were often one-room cabins.

One bachelor U.S. commissioner, who was not the best of housekeepers, commonly had to clean off his kitchen table of dirty dishes and food to have enough room for his typewriter before convening court.

Under such conditions it was necessary for wardens to work closely with the commissioners in his district because they held the key to his enforcement endeavors. It was important that the people understood the judiciary system and the reasons for penalties for misdemeanors. We tried to impress on the Native people at these hearings that we (the wardens) were the ones representing the wildlife that were illegally taken. Our goal was voluntary compliance by hunters, fishermen, and trappers through education.

The offender was usually flown from his village, trapline, or camp, to the commissioner, and at times this meant several hundred miles of flying. At the completion of the hearing, we would fly the offenders back to where they were picked up, unless the comissioner imposed jail time, in which case they were flown to Fairbanks or Anchorage. At times we flew the commissioner to the village where the offender lived and held the hearing in the school or any suitable building where the villagers could attend. In this manner, they become aware of the system and the consequences for the illegal taking of wildlife.

It may not have been the best possible system, but it worked as long as everyone did his part. I spent my time with the commissioners in the McGrath district explaining the reasons for regulations that to the uninitiated appeared capricious or at times ridiculous.

For example, new commissioners wondered why the Alaska

game commission outlawed traps for fish and nets for the taking of fur animals. To anyone familiar with this method of taking mink in the Yukon-Kuskokwim delta, it was an obvious attempt to stop the loss of animals in untended traps. Without experiencing the problem, though, the regulation made little sense.

Eskimos of the delta long ago found that mink entered their blackfish traps in search of food, and that they were more easily taken this way than with steel traps. These fish traps were originally built from willow strips woven into the typical fyke trap, which has a funnel entrance, making it easy to enter, but difficult to get out. The typical blackfish trap is about 36 inches long and about the diameter of a basketball. These traps are set under the ice in back eddies of rivers or streams connecting lakes where blackfish congregate in large numbers.

Alaska blackfish are found in tundra lakes in northern and western Alaska. When the lakes freeze, schools of these prehistoric fish are capable of keeping the ice from freezing around small pools by their continual thrashing. In extreme cold, if the thrashing fails, many of the fish will migrate to streams, while others burrow into the mud for the winter.

Eskimos trap the fish as food for themselves and their dogs. They are also a source of food for mink — and Yukon-Kuskokwim delta mink are the largest, darkest, and best-furred mink in North America. When the trapper sets his blackfish trap it becomes self-baiting, and a one-way enclosure for these valuable furbearers.

So far, no problem; whoever caught the first mink by this method probably felt he had discovered the ultimate trap, and he was close to being right. Eventually these traps were made out of hardware cloth, and it was not an uncommon sight when I patrolled the delta to see loads of them stacked on trappers' dog sleds leaving the village bound for trapping grounds.

Concern over these devices was not with the traps themselves, but rather in the way they were attended. Tundra blizzards have a way of changing treeless barrens, challenging even the most experienced in locating landmarks and trails. As a result, many of the traps were lost. Often trappers lost interest in fighting the elements, especially during and after the winter holiday season, and many would not pick up their traps. Unfortunately, the untended traps continued to self-bait with blackfish, and mink continued to enter them in pursuit of food. The result was wasted mink.

I received complaints from villagers and traders about lost or abandoned traps they had found that contained the rotted carcasses of from one to three mink, and it was this waste that brought about the regulation by the Alaska game commission that made illegal the use of fish traps for taking fur animals.

For a time a regulation was attempted that required a built-in escape hatch for the mink but not the fish, thus making it a true fish trap. "Fish traps commonly used near the Bering Sea coast and adjacent streams for taking blackfish, pike, ling and whitefish shall be provided with a top well of not less than 10 inches in diameter as to allow the escape of any fur animal which may have entered the trap," read Regulation 14 in 1939-40.

But this failed. Trappers weren't interested in letting mink escape, and it was difficult for wardens to locate traps and identify owners. Finally the game commissioners outlawed them. Nets were used in the same manner, and they were also deemed illegal.

I held many village meetings concerning the traps, all to no avail. They were too efficient and easier to use than steel leghold traps. They are still used extensively. Since no one has ever devised a method of controlling abandoned traps, the loss is presumably still a big factor in the mink take of the Yukon-Kuskokwim delta country.

Explaining these and other regulations to the U.S. commissioners, district court judges and U.S. attorneys was a challenge at times, but it had to be done. If they didn't understand the purpose of the regulations they would often dismiss cases which we felt were important to game management.

Another sticky problem for the bush warden was the conflict between the territorial legislature and the FWS concerning the bounty on wolves, coyotes, wolverines, and bald eagles. While the FWS had no problem with the bounty system for wolves and coyotes, it objected to a system which subsidized trappers for taking bald eagles, our national bird, which had complete protection in the lower 48 states, and wolverine, which wasn't considered to be a predator detrimental to game populations.

As a means of combatting the undesirable bounty on wolverine, in 1956 the Alaska game commission included the wolverine in the regulatory trapping season with mink, marten, land otter, fox, lynx and weasel. As a side note, eagles came under full protection of the Migratory Bird Treaty Act after statehood in 1959.

Having much of the year closed to the taking of wolverine caused problems, especially in rural areas where Natives had trouble understanding the logic of regulations anyway. To claim bounties, trappers had to submit the hide of the animal with the left foreleg attached, along with a signed affidavit giving the date and place the bountied animal was taken. Since there were no territorial wildlife officers, FWS agents were delegated to certify bounty claims. We did this by checking out the affidavit, removing the leg bone, and signing off that we had completed the check. Most of the certifications were taken care of in the villages or at trappers' cabins as we traveled. Others were mailed to our offices at Fairbanks, Anchorage, or Juneau where the leg bone was removed, the affidavit certified and the hide mailed back to the owner.

The rub came when an unknowing trapper sent the hide of a wolverine, with the affidavit, to the regional office in Juneau. Often the date given for taking the animal was not within the legal season. While it didn't matter to the dead wolverine or occur to the trapper doing his part in removing predators that there must be a problem (else why would there be a bounty?), it did to administrators. The hide and affidavit were sent to the agent in charge of the district where the animal was taken as an "open case" — an illegally taken animal. We had no choice but to locate the trapper and have him sign a release to all claims to the bounty and to the wolverine hide which became the property of the U.S. government. Most of these honest but illegal claims were sent from remote villages where many of the older people still had a great sense of pride in their way of life. The majority shunned welfare, feeling that the land provided their living and give-away programs were for the lazy.

This was one of the most difficult and unpalatable parts of my job. The letter of the law had to be enforced, yet it served no useful purpose. The rural people were basically honest and they filled out all government forms as truthfully as possible and with pride. They were caught between two opposing philosophies, one dealing with wildlife management and the other (the bounty system) a political measure that was nothing more than a welfare system that had little effect on predator numbers.

An insight into a typical summer patrol was included in Peter Matthiessen's book *Wildlife in America,* published in 1959 by the Viking Press. Mr. Matthiessen was the guest of the FWS in 1957, and traveled throughout the territory with our agents to view firsthand the status of wildlife in Alaska. He traveled with me for several days, making observations and taking copious notes. We made one stop at the village of Eek on the lower Kuskokwim River to take care of an improperly bountied wolverine skin. His comments follow:

... the Service, especially in the law-enforcement branch, remains woefully undermanned. The game agent for the western Interior, for example, must patrol alone an area larger than New England, including the whole Yukon-Kuskokwim delta, and a sketch here of a typical mission in his ceaseless surveillance of the region will give some idea of the task confronting wildlife agents in Alaska. One must keep in mind that, in addition to their ordinary duties, these men perform the functions of the game wardens in the older states.

The delta formed between the mouths of the Yukon and Kuskokwim is a remote foggy world of dark tundra pools, bleak, faceless shore, and isolated volcanic peaks rising mysteriously above the waste; its wilderness of water rivals the sloughs and potholes of the Canadian prairie provinces as the great North American nesting grounds for waterfowl, though only a relatively narrow strip behind the beach is heavily populated by the birds. While the Canadian grounds favor ducks over geese, the reverse is true on the Yukon-Kuskokwim, and emperor, white-fronted, and cackling geese, in company with large numbers of whistling swans, are the dominant birds. There are black brant, too, and a variety of ducks, including such sea ducks as eider and old-squaw, as well as innumerable lesser sandhill cranes, shore birds, jaegers, and gulls.

The land, relentlessly monotone in all but a few summer weeks of feverish flowering, is almost uninhabited. The distances are so great that the game agent must fly endless rounds in suitable weather if he is to touch at each scattered Eskimo settlement and fishing camp even once a year. Much of the work can be done only in season, when the waters are free of ice. On the rare clear days the fishing camps on the outer deltas may be detected from a distance by the red racks of drying salmon and the flapping of white canvas tents, but at other times there are no landmarks, only the black faces of the ponds shifting evilly in the Bering mists. Poor flying weather may ground the agent for many days at a time.

Nor are the natives always glad to see him. They line up silently on the river bank as he sets his pontoons on the roiled waters, the ceaseless wind stirring the fur trim on the parkas. The agent singles out the village leader and tells the purpose of his visit. Gently, insistently, almost apologetically, he confiscates a wolverine pelt submitted for bounty out of season, then lectures the round-faced, resigned group on the waterfowl laws which preserve sport shooting for the white man in faraway America. Since the waterfowl, for them, may mean survival, they cannot be expected to understand the laws, and the agent does not really expect them to obey. Apologizing in their turn, they tell him again as they had told him the year before that they must take the geese in early spring if they are not to starve before the great silver king salmon makes its run in from the sea. One says he is proud to be an American and to obey the American law, but that his children must be allowed to eat; he offers to tell the agent how often the law is broken here, if that will be of service to the government, but he repeats.that it will be broken. The agent counsels them obliquely against waste, repeats the letter of the law, and smiles. Immediately the fishermen smile, too, and remember the pidgin English they had forgotten so long as his presence posed a threat. One asks him in a sing-song voice, "Why is it the birds go away so many in the fall of the year, and come back to us so few?" And the agent patiently explains, using his hands. Like all the Service personnel one meets in remote places, he is dedicated, and does not begrudge his time.

I found Matthiessen's unbiased view rewarding, especially his comments on the wolverine skin, which I considered to be a routine but unjustifiable part of the job.

A human population explosion has taken place on the Yukon-Kuskokwim delta since I patrolled the area as a game warden. Today there are about 20,000 persons, mostly Eskimos, living in 55 villages there. The delta is relatively productive of wildlife, in common with deltas the world around, but hunting and fishing pressures, high in the 1950s, have today reached almost unbearable proportions. Almost any moose that wanders onto the delta is immediately shot. Spring hunting and egg taking is having a serious impact on certain species of waterfowl, including cackling, lesser Canada, brant and white-fronted geese.

The state is now embroiled in an Alaska-wide "subsistence rights" controversy which promises to separate Alaskans for generations to come. What was once simple is now complex. One wonders if the wildlife will survive until the powers that be decide who have the rights to its use.

Unlike the two trappers and the beaver houses, it seems we cannot split anything 50-50 any more: It is all or nothing.■

Chapter 2

Preseason Trapline Patrols

T HE TRAPPING SEASON in Interior Alaska for marten, mink, land otter, fox, lynx and weasel in the 1950s extended from November 16 through January 31. These furbearers could be taken by any means except by use of a set gun, a shotgun, artificial light or traps with jaws having a spread exceeding 9 inches. Nor were poisons, dogs, chemicals, fish traps or smoke allowed. Traps could not be set within 100 feet of a fox den and homes, houses or dens were not to be disturbed.

The reason for the season's beginning and ending dates was to assure pelt primeness. The game commission, backed by years of experience and studies that had been conducted by Fish and Wildlife Service biologists, believed that fur animals should only be taken when they were the most valuable, and not before or after. Skins taken early are thin and have few guard hairs, and the hide is blue, indicating that the hair roots are not fully set. After the end of January the longer guard hairs tend to become singed and split, also making them less desirable.

The other regulations were provided to prohibit methods that would be detrimental to the resource, other wildlife or to humans through the misuse of poison or traps. Disrupting homes and dens is self-explanatory, and the use of smoke and chemicals was prohibited because many animals suffocated in their dens and could not be retrieved. It was also considered inhumane.

Trapping was still an important means of maintaining an existence for many people and the only way for some, especially Natives, for providing a livelihood for their families. As with any other occupaton, there were those who cheated. Some advanced the season because it was easier trapping during the warm weather, and even though the fur was not fully prime and brought low prices many felt quantity versus quality would put them ahead in money. Others that trapped near villages, trapped early to beat out competitors. Some broke the law just because they believed it was their right to take wildlife whenever and wherever they felt like it. Others were just inefficient or lazy.

It was our job to assure that those who took furs did so in accordance with regulations. Having been a trapper several years and developing pride in the profession, I took a special interest in this part of my job.

Normally, Interior Alaska's lakes froze over by November 1 and enabled us to use ski-equipped aircraft. This gave us two weeks to check for illegal trapping activities before the season opened. Because the fur-producing areas were so vast we picked one section of the district and concentrated our efforts there. If extensive violations were found, we went back to the same area the following year to determine if our efforts had had a deterring effect. If not, we worked the area again, oftentimes picking up the same violators a second time.

A typical patrol would have us operating out of a centrally located village that had a roadhouse and gas facilities. Before dawn we would be out heating the aircraft with a plumber's firepot. After the firepot was primed and generating a good blue flame, it was put inside of the canvas engine cover which covered the cowling and prop. The engine cover draped to the ground, which in effect formed a tent around the front of the plane. The firepot was set on the ground beneath the engine and before long the inside of the engine cover was warmed and the thawing process began. When it was below zero the engine would turn white and slowly the frost would melt and drip. The warming was continued until the prop could be turned freely. (At -30° or lower it can't be budged). The oil which had been drained the night before and kept warm was poured back into the engine. Depending on the temperature, it took from 30 minutes to an hour to prepare the engine. The wing covers installed the night before to keep frost from building up on the wings were removed while the engine thawed. At last the engine was started and allowed to run until all the gauges said it was a go. At this point we put the engine cover back on to keep the engine warm and went back to the roadhouse to eat breakfast.

I was bemoaning the problems of this long, drawn-out

procedure one day to Hutch, an old-time mechanic who maintained our aircraft in Fairbanks. He listened patiently as I mentioned what a time-consuming chore it was to put on wing covers, drain the oil and secure the aircraft at night, especially when we had to cut tie downs in the lake or river ice. In the morning we agonized with the firepot, especially with the Gullwing Stinson which required two firepots because the nose was so high in the air. One of us had to stand beside the engine cover to make sure the wind did not blow the canvas into the flame and that the firepot did not go out, shooting raw gas into the air. (Many a plane was lost due to carelessness on the part of the pilot who decided to get a cup of coffee during this operation.) It seemed as if we spent more time taking care of the airplane on the ground than we did flying it.

When I was finished, Hutch grinned and said, "You young fellers sure have it easy. When I was doing this years ago we had water cooled engines and had to take the oil and radiator water inside to warm."

What a balloon buster! After that I chose my audiences more carefully.

Now I can throw my weight around with the modern bush pilots because everyone today has insulated engine covers. Just wrap one around the engine and plug in an electric heater or fit a thermax heater inside the cowling and everything is nice and toasty warm in the morning. Young guys today don't know what tough is.

When it was full daylight we started patrolling dog team trails. By flying low and reading the tracks we were able to determine what activities the traveler was up to and could plan our work accordingly. Often the trapper was supplying his camps for the season or checking fur sign, and being satisfied that he was legally engaged we moved to another line. If, on the other hand, the tracks indicated that traps were being set, we had to land and walk out parts of the line. At times this proved most difficult, especially when the only place to land was a lake, slough or river several miles from the trapline. Often I would land at one end of the line, drop off my partner, and then proceed to another part of the line where we would later meet. There were occasions when we would take our packs, snowshoes and sleeping bags and walk out different parts of a line, returning to the plane several days later. These excursions were undertaken only when we had a particularly active poacher who was savvy enough to set his traps miles from any place a plane could land. These fellows were difficult to catch without a lot of planning and hard work. Many times I walked miles of line wondering if I was tracking an honest trapper only to find an illegally killed moose or caribou used as bait or a string of traps set in dense timber to remain undetected from the air. Yet there were times when the trapper was completely legal, which was rewarding, and we would leave him a note congratulating him on his legal operations.

One year early in my career, one of our deputy agents, Dave Lanni, and I worked out of my old trapping cabin at Lake Minchumina. We were trying to locate several trappers who had been reported trapping illegally in the Nowitna River area. From the air we found one line that was over 60 miles long. With no place to land within walking distance of the trail, we backtracked it to the main cabin. This trapper was smarter than most, and if he had any traps, it would require several days of traveling on foot to determine what he was up to. By this time darkness was fast approaching and a threatening snow storm was reducing the visibility considerably. It would be a night of siwashing unless we found a cabin to use. We circled the trapper's cabin situated on the bank of the river and found no smoke or other sign of life. We were leary of landing on the river ice because we had no idea if it would support the weight of the airplane. We looked over a small pothole lake about 500 yards away and we made several passes to check the length and ice conditions. Shortly, the weather began snowing heavily and the sky darkened by the minute. We lined up with the longest section and "floundered" in for a landing. I say floundered because when we came in over the trees we realized they were much taller than they had appeared in the restricted visibility, and we had to do some not-too-fancy maneuvers to get the plane down before running out of lake and crashing into the bank on the other end. It turned out to be a "controlled crash,"complete with a slalom ski turn at the end. Once we had shut down and looked around we realized that we'd have one heck of a time getting back out of this hole. The trees were 75 to 100 feet high with a 10 foot bank and in the now complete darkness they looked formidable, to say the least. We drained the oil and put on the wing covers without much small talk and packed our gear to the cabin.

The cabin showed signs of use, with two sets of moose quarters hanging on a meat pole in the back and dirty dishes on the table. It was obviously being used by the trapper and his Indian wife, who had come up by boat before freeze-up with the intention of staying all winter. We cooked up a meal from our grub sack and played a few games of gin rummy before turning in without mentioning the size of the lake we had landed on or how we were going to get out in the morning. Finally, we threw our sleeping bags on the bunk, which had a mattress of layered grass, and called it a day. I spent a fitfull night of nightmares. Each was the same: I would try to fly the plane out of the small lake and end up crashing into the trees at the other

end. To add to the zest of the nightmares, there were mice living in the straw, and they kept running around searching for food. One got into my hair, causing me to sit upright and start slapping the bedding with a stick to rid me of the pesky critters. All Dave could say was, "It's the pits ain't it," and pull down into his bag like a caterpillar in a cocoon. Nothing worked for me, though, and between the mice and the crashes in my dreams, I might just have well stayed up all night.

I finally got up about 5 a.m. and made a pot of coffee. While I was waiting for it to boil, I looked around and behind the stove in a box I found a cow moose head. Indians enjoy eating the nose of a moose. This head had been skinned and the nose obviously had been consumed. I showed the head to Dave and indicated that obviously one of the moose on the meat rack must be a cow. When it became daylight we went out and examined the meat pole that we had casually observed the night before in the dark. We were not happy with what we found. The quarters were all uncovered and a few appeared to have soured. The birds had been busy and had eaten big holes in the meat before it froze. They had also defecated over the meat, leaving it a deplorable mess. Pictures were taken and we decided to bring the head back to town as evidence. We would discuss the taking of the cow and the waste of meat with the U.S. attorney. Back in the cabin we did the dishes, cleaned the cabin and gathered our gear together. I grabbed an ax and we went out to the river to test the thickness of the ice. Several test holes showed that it was about 5 inches deep, which was plenty adequate to support the aircraft, so we marked off a runway on the smoothest portion. The plan was that I would take off empty from the lake and pick up Dave and the gear on the river. On the walk back to the lake with the warm oil I kept thinking of my nightmares and wondering if it was a bad omen or if I was letting my imagination get the best of me. Once at the lake I realized that I had reason to be concerned because it was small and the banks and trees were definitely obstacles to be reckoned with. I walked it all out as Dave firepotted and made sure there was no overflow to slow down the skis. Then I paced it off and determined the direction that would give me the longest takeoff run. When all this was accomplished I warmed up the engine and taxied to the far end where Dave and I pulled the tail back as far as it would go against the bank. Looking ahead was not encouraging but it was bite the bullet, firewall the throttle, and coax the plane to its limits. I remembered the old axiom that says "Use up all the available runway and pull it off, then if you don't make it, it's the airplane's fault." I did just that and at the end popped the flaps and exchanged airspeed for altitude, and lo and behold, we jumped over the trees without any shocking, shuttering or stalling. Nothing to it I remember shouting, but my sweaty palms and the rivulets running down my forehead told a different story. The shout was just relieving a lot of inside tension. The rest was academic, and we were on our way without being able to check out the trapper's line for the year. The legal season would open too soon.

I picked up Dave and the gear, and we proceeded up the Sulatna River. We cut a trail and followed it back to a cabin just as a dog team was arriving. Landing on the river we made contact with the young trapper as he was unhitching his dogs. The first thing that I noticed was some skinned marten carcasses on the roof of the cabin which the trapper hadn't fed to his dogs yet. After several minutes of questioning he admitted to trapping early and produced the illegal marten and mink skins. Because of the distance involved to his home village of Ruby, I requested that he pull up all of his traps and meet us there in 10 days to answer to the charges I would file before the U.S. commissioner for taking fur animals during the closed season. I used this method of apprehension successfully throughout the years I worked in the field for non-aggrevated violations. The violator could take care of his dog team or have another trapper or someone in a village care for them in the event he had to be taken to town. He agreed and we took off and continued our patrol effort. We checked several more lines picking up a few traps before proceeding to Minchumina that night and Fairbanks the following day.

The next two days were spent writing up reports on the patrol and preparing complaints to be filed with the different U. S. commissioners. Then two things occurred that changed my plans considerably for the next few days.

The first was a message I heard while listening to "Tundra Topics" during the third evening I was home. "Tundra Topics" was a program sponsored by a local radio station that allowed people to send messages to friends or relatives in the Bush who had no other method of communication. Usually it was someone advising when they were arriving for a visit or to expect a shipment by plane on a certain day. There were important messages about births, deaths and people in the hospital as well as the general interest messages like the one that really caught my attention. It was from a trapper and his wife on the Nowitna River to their friends in Ruby. It seemed that a local bush pilot had landed at their camp to deliver provisions and check on their welfare. Through him they delivered their message to the radio station that day. In effect it said that Billy and Mary had arrived at their trapping camp late in September by boat. All was well, and the only incident of concern had happened a few weeks before. Mary had been charged by a cow moose, and it had to be shot. They had salvaged the meat, but could not turn it over to the Fish and Wildlife Service due to their isolation. So they would utilize it as best they could. I thought about the cow moose head in the evidence locker and realized that I had been beat. It was obvious that the story was a fabrication; however, it had merit and that was all that counted.

The next day I took the head to the dump thinking to myself that sometimes you win and sometimes you lose. I had just lost this one. I was learning.

Later that afternoon another occurence took place that significantly changed the previous week's events. Mike McRoberts, deputy U.S. marshal, came to the office requesting information. He was trying to locate someone trapping in the Ruby area who was wanted for robberies in Fairbanks. The thief had been nicknamed the "Blue Parka Bandit" because he wore a blue parka and a handkerchief mask. I was surprised to learn the suspect was the trapper we had apprehended on the Sulatna River due in Ruby in seven days. That is if he were going to follow directions. Could I find him again, was the question. We decided to leave as early as possible.

We departed before daylight the next morning and flew directly to Ruby. An inquiry in the village determined that the trapper had not returned, so we flew to the Sulatna River. A pass over the cabin showed it to be empty, so we followed his trails and located him about 20 miles out in the opposite direction from the trail to Ruby. Either he was still trapping or he was pulling traps. My guess was that he was still trapping, but there was no place to land and determine this. Somehow we had to find a way to approach without alerting him to the fact that he was to be arrested, otherwise he could play a cat and mouse game out in the woods indefinitely. We decided that the best plan was to drop Mike off at his cabin and I would go back to Ruby, returning in the morning. We circled the dog team once more then took a direct heading for Ruby. After five minutes we felt he would no longer be able to hear the aircraft engine, and we circled back just over tree top level to land at the cabin. I dropped off Mike with his sleeping bag and grub and headed back to Ruby for the night.

The next morning I heated the airplane and departed for the cabin. I circled, and after Mike gave me the sign that he had made the arrest, I landed. The suspect was in handcuffs and I told him we would leave his dogs behind but fly back with someone to drive them to his house. He gave me the name of his friend who would do this for him, and I went back to Ruby alone, contacted the man and flew him to the cabin with his gear. Then Mike, the trapper and I flew to Fairbanks. The next day he was taken before the U.S. commissioner and sentenced to

50 days in jail for illegal trapping. Later, faced with the evidence against him, the trapper confessed to three armed robberies, which netted him four years in a reformatory.

Sometimes you win, sometimes you lose. This time we won.

Chapter 3

LAWLESS VALLEY

M Y SUMMARY OF THE McGrath district operations for March 1958 ended with this paragraph:

> A short trip to Fairbanks was made with U.S. Commissioner Dave Leach from Aniak to confer with District Judge Vernon Forbes. Assistance was given to the judge and clerk of court in determining a new boundary for the Aniak Precinct. Conferred with U.S. Marshal Al Dorsch about "Lawless Valley," a name given the Kuskokwim River area, which is again without a deputy marshal at Bethel or McGrath. Mr. Dorsch suggested this agent accept an appointment as honorary deputy marshal, but the offer was declined as it was felt that the new uniform would sag and bag under the weight of *two* badges.

I had been detailed to McGrath in June of 1956 to take charge of the district, which included all the drainages of the Kuskokwim River, the Yukon River and its drainages south of Kaltag and all the coastal areas from Unalakleet south to Goodnews Bay, including Nunivak Island. At that time, there was one deputy marshal stationed at McGrath and another at Bethel to cover the same district. In territorial days, the Marshal's office handled most of the major crime problems and transportation of prisoners in the outlying areas. There was some overlap with the territorial police authorities. However, the area in question was so large that there were seldom jurisdictional problems.

Compared with today's standards, the area was quite peaceful, with relatively few crimes. There were occasional murders, rapes and disorderly conduct that were mostly alcohol related, but for the most part, the marshals had it easy. We often worked together and coordinated patrols, and I became quite familiar with their profession. They would often call for assistance in hauling prisoners or to transport back to town the bodies of trappers who died during the winter on traplines.

By 1958 the territorial police were assuming more of the responsibility for responding to emergency complaints of crime in the villages. The marshal's office was kept busy in the larger cities as court bailiff, process server, and escort for prisoners going to federal prisons outside Alaska.

The police had a major problem; they were working with a limited budget and could only react to emergencies. None were stationed in the villages, so there was always a delay in getting to the troubled areas due to travel problems. Here again, I made myself available and assisted whenever needed because I was continually traveling throughout the district and was in effect the only law enforcement official in that part of a Alaska.

U.S. commissioners were appointed by federal judges for each judicial district and were ex officio justices of the peace. Court was held wherever convenient. Some had a room set aside in their home, but others used the living room, kitchen or any room that was available. One commissioner traveled with me during a spring season when there was a considerable number of trappers taking beaver illegally. Most were taking more than the legal limit of 10, planning to have someone in the village seal them and split the profits. With the commissioner available at the scene, I filed complaints and court was held in the trapper's tent, or at times, outside, using a log as a bench. Most often when there was a problem in a village, the commissioner was transported to the locale, and a trial held at the completion of the investigation. In the case of a serious crime, a jury was selected and the local school or meeting hall was used for the proceedings. Justice for the most part was fair and seldom did anyone complain of being railroaded. None of the commissioners that I was associated with had law degrees or any formal schooling in law, but all had a great deal of common sense which prevailed when sentences were imposed. The enforcement officers did the investigation, filed the complaints and acted as prosecuting attorney. Compared with these days of complicated laws and court proceedings, the system was simple, effective and respected throughout the Territory.

A typical request for assistance came from Sgt. Emery Chapple, territorial police at Fairbanks, who needed assistance and transportation to Kaltag to investigate a rape complaint. I departed McGrath in the Fish & Wildlife Service, float-equipped,

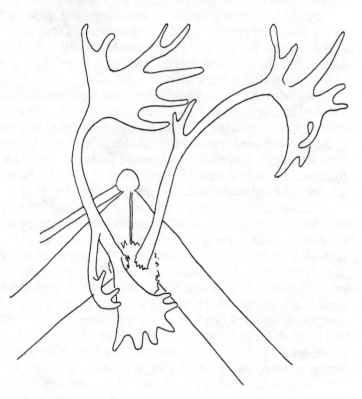

Cessna 180 and flew to Galena. There I picked up Emery, who had arrived via Northern Consolidated Airlines. We proceeded to Kaltag where a trial was held. After the trial the commissioner was flown back to Ruby, and Emery and I went to Koyukuk for the night.

I felt fortunate that we landed before dark because the rivers were extremely high, with a considerable amount of debris and trees being carried by the main current. With a long day behind us and the plane secured, we settled in for a pleasant evening of socializing with the Vernettis, who owned the trading post.

Our peace and tranquility ended abruptly when an Indian man, who had split his foot open with an ax while cutting wood, was brought in. We administered first aid, but it was apparent that he needed emergency medical attention that could not wait until morning.

The closest facility was the military base at Galena 50 miles up river so we packed him into the plane and departed. At Galena, after radioing for assistance, I landed in the Yukon River on the opposite side from the village to stay out of the main channel and avoid hitting any logs. We taxied in slowly, threading our way through the debris with the use of the taxi light. When we got beached we transferred the patient to a waiting vehicle. With that part of the operation successfully accomplished, we now had to get back to Koyukuk because at Galena there was no place to tie up a float plane to protect it from the river.

By taxiing back through the main channel I was able to take off in the slack water where we had landed without incident. Landing in the Koyukuk River was a different situation, however, because it was much narrower and there was no slack water. A long approach was made with the landing light on as I dragged the water looking for an opening in the drift. Finally, I plopped it in and we held our breath hoping we wouldn't hit a big log or tree stump. We lucked out and with a big sigh of relief, tied up in front of the trading post. This time we did get to relax and got a good night's sleep.

The next morning we were to proceed back to Kaltag. There we would pick up the prisoner from yesterday's trial who was being held in custody by a paid guard and go back to Galena. Then we would split: Emery and the prisoner would go to Fairbanks by airline, and I would go back to McGrath.

When I went out to the plane I found it listing to the right. Further examination showed a punctured float. In the black of night we had tied the aircraft up by turning it around and setting the heels on the bank as high as we could pull them. What we hadn't known was that the main compartment had been dragged over an old boat engine that had been left there years earlier and was now covered by the high water. This was a major setback since there was no way to take off without patching the hole and to do that required getting the float out of the water.

One thing that was always available in most villages was assistance, and we didn't lack for help at Koyukuk. Planks and timbers showed up, and with several men pushing and others pulling, we slid the problem float out of the water where we could work on it. After drying the damaged area with a blow torch, a temporary patch was applied. When set back in the water the patch held, but a slow leak was still evident. The trip was completed by pumping the float before each takeoff, and Emery and his prisoner were delivered to Galena.

I headed back to McGrath for a change of clothes and a float pumping, then on to Anchorage for a permanent patch to the float. When I returned it was for another change of clothes and a tour of all the villages, delivering the new hunting, fishing and trapping regulations. As I left, my wife reminded me that it might be nice if I stayed home long enough to introduce myself to the children again so they wouldn't forget who I was. My answer was simple: Get Marshal Dorsch to put some deputies at McGrath and Bethel and allow me to just do my work as a wildlife enforcement agent! ■

Chapter 4

The Gullwing
Stinson

T HE 'GULLWING' IS MY AIRPLANE. I shall not rest,"so said
Sig Olson in his poem *Ode to the Gullwing* (with apologies
to King David). Sig, a good friend and biologist for the U.S. Fish
and Wildlife Service, wrote the poem after our many adventures
with old N782.

When I checked out in the Stinson the summer of 1953,
I felt that I had reached the peak of my flying career. The big
five-place aircraft, boasting a round 300 Lycoming engine,
constant speed prop, and graceful wings, had for years proven
itself to be a reliable bush plane in Alaska. As the gullwing had
established its credibility, so I was eager to prove mine, and a
great love affair was born that lasted until she was sold in 1961.
We flew together over all of northern Alaska on enforcement
patrols, game counts, freight hauls and trips for V.I.P.'s to observe
firsthand the many facets of Alaska's game management
problems. On one trip with Ray Woolford and Walt Ahmaoyak,
we flew a considerable distance north of Point Barrow over the
pack ice to make polar bear observations. I learned a valuable
lesson in radio navigation on that trip, as well as the Eskimo
method of traveling without the aid of a compass.

We had flown several hours north of the most northerly tip
of Alaska making notes of ice pack conditions and the numbers
of polar bears. When we found a fresh track we followed it until
we found the bear, made notes of direction of travel and recorded
any seal kills in the vicinity. When we were down to two hours
fuel we decided it was time to head back to Barrow. I tuned on
the plane's aircraft directional finder and after the needle settled
down, headed in the direction it pointed. After about an hour

of droning along, Walt, who was sitting in the co-pilot's seat, asked where I was going. When I said Point Barrow, he pointed to the right about 90 degrees and said it was that way. I explained to him how the ADF worked and how once the receiver was tuned, the needle would point to the station, and for all practical purposes you just had to follow it home. I did not go into correcting for wind drift since we were not encountering any problems. He listened patiently and shook his head saying he didn't know anything about the gadget I was following but, "Barrow that way," pointing right again.

Ray Woolford, who was in the back seat, poked his head between us and looked at the ADF, listened to Walt and then asked me for the radio headset. After a few minutes he smiled, gave me back the headset and said, "You're not tuned to Barrow." Stunned, I listened myself to the morse code identifier and sure enough, I had tuned in Barter Island. I had committed the cardinal sin of not positively identifying the station before turning on the homing switch of the receiver. This meant we were paralleling the coast about 150 miles out and with our limited gas supply would have never reached land, a stupid mistake that could have been costly if it hadn't been for Walt. I properly tuned the radio and the needle swung to the right just where Walt was pointing, and when I turned in that direction, he smiled and we all relaxed again.

We arrived at Barrow about an hour later with little fuel remaining. After we secured the plane I questioned Walt on how he knew we were going in the wrong direction. He told me that the predominant winds in this part of the world are northeast-southwest and the snow on the non-moving ice always formed hard drifts in those directions. This was the way Eskimos navigated on the ice on hunting trips many miles from land. They cut the drifts at a certain angle on the way out and reversed the procedure back.

I had learned two valuable lessons on that trip. The first was to positively identify the station being used for navigational purposes, which is so necessary, especially in instrument flying. The other was how to keep track of directions on the ice pack by using the wind drifts as a guide. I have used the example on radio tuning many times in teaching students to fly, but have never had occasion to use the second.

Although this was not the only time the old girl humbled

me, we always accomplished our missions with nary a scratch to her fuselage. There was the time I was asked to fly some Canadian dignitaries north of Fairbanks to observe the caribou calving grounds. It was June 3, 1955, and a science conference was being held at the University of Alaska. Biologists from several countries were presenting wildlife research papers at the conference and a major topic was the Alaska-Canada caribou herds. It seemed that the Canadians had lost a major segment of their herd in the Yukon and Northwest Territories while Alaska was enjoying a great abundance of the critters. The migration patterns of these travelers were being studied by several teams from both countries. There was a great deal of speculation that they traveled great distances back and forth across the border, giving them dual citizenship. This, of course, has been confirmed and the movements of the different herds is now well established.

Frank Banfield, Canada's caribou expert, and two of his colleagues were my passengers. Sig Olson rode in the co-pilot's seat to act as guide and tour director. We were to fly to the Preacher Creek area of the White Mountains to observe the large number of caribou and calves in that area.

The gullwing was parked at Fairbanks International Airport, which had just been opened the year before. The only building was the CAA tower and we had permission to park on the apron just opposite that stucture. I had done a complete pre-flight prior to the arrival of the biologists so I invited them to climb aboard as they walked up to the plane. There is only one door on this aircraft, and it is aft of the wing strut on the left side. If the rear passengers get in first, which was usually the case, the pilot and the person who sits in the right seat have to watch their step as they make their way up between the two front seats. Somebody's feet were always getting stepped on, so I made it a habit to make sure everything was a go before getting in last.

After everyone was settled I cranked up the engine and allowed it to warm up as I monitored the gauges. Since my passengers were not pilots I was naturally going to impress them with my flying skills, so I activated the switch making all radio transmissions audible on the overhead speaker. I was sure they would be interested in hearing me talk to the tower operator and to the Fish and Wildlife Service secretary monitoring us on the radio. I would file a flight plan with her and keep her advised periodically of our progress.

After everything was ready, I called the tower in my most professional voice, "Fairbanks tower this is Stinson N782 parked in front of the tower and ready to taxi." The operator answered, "N782 cleared to taxi to runway 19, wind calm, suggest you untie your wings first."

Talk about eating humble pie! I had to shut down the engine and step on everyone's feet climbing out to release the tie down ropes. So much for impressing my passengers. I'm surprised they opted to continue the flight. They were obviously very dedicated scientists.

Experienced pilots had a saying about Stinsons, "They're built like a bridge and they fly like one." This was true. They were one of the strongest planes ever constructed, but they were ground lovers. It was not a short field aircraft, but once airborne they were a great comfort, especially while flying in turbulence. The stout gear was also appreciated when landing on rough, rocky runways or when botching the touchdown. I did a good job of proving this point one night during the fall hunting season in 1954.

We had set up a check station at Paxson that year to keep track of the harvest of moose and caribou along the newly opened Denali Highway. Several temporary employees were hired to man the trailer that was set up at the junction of the Denali and Richardson Highways. I was assisting this effort by making daily flights in the gullwing to make sure no hunters were camped in closed areas. The airstrip paralleled the road and was about 1,500 feet long, crowned by a hill on the north end. This significant obstacle prompted takeoffs to the south and landings being made to the north with the Stinson.

Two fellows had to be flown to Healy one evening to assist with some problems that had developed in that neighborhood. This meant a late return flight and I knew I would be arriving after dark. The only possible landing would be toward the hill and touchdown would have to be precise on the first part of the strip. To add zest to this adventure, the landing light was not working.

Before departing, I requested one of the temporary workers put a gas lantern on the exact end of the usable runway on the left hand corner, which would act as a guide for my descent and landing.

As anticipated, it was quite dark when I returned and after several passes, the lantern appeared and finally became stationary at the end of the field.

I made a long approach with my eyes on the lantern, came up even with it, chopped the power and hauled back on the stick ready for touchdown. Suddenly, a sickening, sinking sensation surged through me as the bottom fell out. The airplane stalled and plunged for what felt like a an eternity before hitting the ground. Needless to say, what was supposed to be a feather-light landing turned into a bone-jarring, soul-quaking crash, which would have destroyed the landing gear on any airplane but that of the gullwing. After gingerly bringing the plane to a halt and finding out how many teeth I had left, if any, I shakily walked back to find out what had happened.

Nothing much, except for the fact that my young friend had really wanted to help me out. To do so, he had attached the gas lantern, my handsome guiding light, to a 20-foot pole which he had then proudly held high into the air above his head. With friends like that who needed enemies? It did prove one thing however: She was a stout ship.

Another feature of this plane that sometimes caused problems was the non-steering tail wheel. Most modern planes have the tail wheel assembly connected to the rudder pedals so that when the rudder is moved right or left while taxiing, the tail wheel follows. This simple tracking mechanism greatly assists in more positive steering on the ground, especially in crosswinds. The fully castored tail gear of the gullwing was easily kept aligned with the use of brakes while the aircraft was on wheels; however, once skis were installed the situation changed considerably. Now the only turning force available was the affect of the propeller blast on the rudder, and when fully loaded in deep snow or glare ice a large area was required to complete a turn.

There were several ways to accomplish this. One was to wrap a rope several turns around the inside ski to slow down the sliding action of that ski which in turn acted as a brake. The big trick was figuring out a knot that did not jam as the rope slid back on the bottom and became taut. Usually the line had to be cut, so good tie down ropes were not used for this purpose. Another big problem with this method was having to get out with the engine running, tie on the rope, get back in and complete the turn, get back out to take the rope off, and then back in to takeoff.

Shutting down the engine would have been safer; however, cold weather starts are hard on an aircraft battery and it was unwise to take the chance of not having enough juice to get the engine going again.

A better method was having a skookum passenger who would get out and push the tail around as you blasted the prop. Volunteers were hard to come by however, because it was a nasty job, especially when the temperature was below zero. The wind chill factor from the propeller required the person to be in his parka with the hood up and wearing his heaviest mittens. Because visibility was restricted due to swirling snow, the pusher could only follow the tail around not really knowing when it was in position for takeoff. The pilot, on the other hand, would have to apply full power to get the plane moving so that inertia

could help move the tail ski in the direction required. Left turns were always planned, if possible, to take advantage of the engine and propeller torque. When the turn was completed it was sometimes necessary to keep the plane moving forward and get aligned in a set of ski tracks or hard packed snow so the skis would break free for takeoff. The pusher working in the blowing snow would oftentimes not know when to quit and sometimes ended up getting knocked over by the horizontal stabilizer. Strained feelings could result if the person did not have a sense of humor, so pushers were chosen carefully and cherished by the pilots.

Sig Olson had many a good story to tell about being on the tail end of the Stinson, and it was he who categorized the positions of the pilots and passengers as the "blasters" and the "pushers."

When we were issued uniforms in 1957, there was some consideration about designing a set of wings to be worn by the pilots. Sig suggested that pushers be considered for a badge of distinction also. His idea was a set of crossed snowshoes with a hashmark on the uniform sleeve for each time the pusher was run over by the tail! In his case, however, it was determined that the sleeve of his coat was not long enough to support that many hashmarks. Sig was definitely our most devoted pusher.

Taxiing on glare ice was expecially tricky, particularly going downwind. The plane wants to weathercock into the wind and go in circles if the breeze is strong enough. The pusher must walk along the back of the aircraft keeping the tail heading in a straight direction.

On one occasion, Ray Wolford and I landed on the lake behind the village of Kobuk. It was spring and the ice was free of snow, making it very slick. When we were ready for departure, Ray asked if I wanted him to walk behind to steer the plane in the 20-knot wind. We had to taxi downwind the full length of the lake, which would be difficult, but I felt I could do it and suggested he get in for a try.

After warming the engine I started very slowly down the middle of the narrow lake. When we had advanced about 100 yards the plane started to veer to the left. There was a split decision to make — either stop and have Ray get out or blast the tail to straighten it out. I chose the latter and gave the engine a good burst of power. Instead of the straightening out, the Stinson swerved even more, gathered momentum and headed off the lake into the willows. I shut down, and Ray's only remark was, "I really didn't mind walking behind, you know." No, I didn't know, and after all, he was my supervisor, and I didn't think it proper for him to be walking the plane in full view of all the villagers that were out to see the takeoff.

Fortunately, the onlookers were a happy bunch, because we were turned 90 degrees to the lake in the dense brush. Only one solution was available — brute force pulling and pushing backwards. After several tries with little effect, some of the men went back to the village and brought back several dog teams and all the available man power. The dogs were hooked up to a long tow line assisted by several of the men. Others pushed on the gear, skis and inboard wing struts. After much yelling and grunting, it moved, and once started, made its way backwards to the center of the lake. Nothing had to be said this time. Ray stayed outside as I cranked up and slowly taxied to the other end of the lake while he walked the tail keeping it from wandering again. His only comment as he climbed back into the airplane was, "Do you suppose, as a pilot, I would have been entitled to a hashmark if I had been back on the tail when you blasted it?" No answer was necessary and the incident wasn't mentioned again except to wonder what we would have done had we been alone when the Stinson decided to head into the brush.

Burt Libby, a graduate student at the University of Alaska Wildlife Research Unit, had an interesting episode. The unit had a contract with the air force to produce a survival manual for pilots. The idea was to catalog plants and animal life in the different parts of Alaska. This manual would be a part of the pilot's kit, and if forced down he cold look into the part of the book for the area he was in and for his survival determine what plant and animal life existed. Burt was in charge of the project under the direction of Dr. John Buckley, the unit leader.

In the spring of the year I had to fly transects that were laid out on a map at random across Interior Alaska, some several hundred miles long. While I held a course following the line on the map, Burt in the co-pilot's seat, and another student sitting behind me, watched the snow very carefully, making observations of tracks, animals and vegetation, dictating them into tape recorders. The flying had to be accurate according to Dr. Buckley; exactly 100 feet over the terrain, covering the distance on the map from the specific starting point to the precise end.

One day we were running a rather long transect that ended in a narrow valley of the Minto hills. As we entered the valley I planned my turn at the exact point on the map where the transect ended, knowing it would be tight. At the right moment I banked sharply to the left, extending the flaps to shorten the steep turn. Just as we started around the engine sputtered. I had neglected to switch gas tanks, and the left one had just run dry. In my confusion (remember the adage — flying is hours and hours of boredom broken up by moments of stark terror) I reached beside my left leg for the selector valve. This was natural reaction, because the day before I had been flying a Piper Pacer and that's where the valve is in it. Lo and behold, no selector valve; it was on the console directly in front of me. My right hand reached up and flipped the valve as we were about to enter the trees, the engine caught and the turn was completed at a very low altitude. (We weren't very high to begin with!) Nothing much was said.

We continued on our way and finished the day's flying. When we were back in the office, we reviewed the tapes to make sure that the recorders had functioned and captured all the details of the transects. I listened attentively for Burt's reaction as the recorded voice reached the point when we were in the canyon. It went something like this, "We're approaching the completion of this transect which ends in a narrow valley. As we climb, the vegetation is changing from willows and black spruce to birch and alder. Tracks of several moose are meandering up the side hill. One moose at the end of the transect. We are in a steep turn, the engine just quit (pause), there, it started again and we're completing the turn rather close to the ground. Now we will continue to transect #33." No emotion, no change in voice pitch, just matter of fact reporting of routine data. I shrugged and thought he's either fearless or has lots of confidence in my piloting. I accepted it as a compliment. Naturally, I chose the latter; no sense both of us being scared.

We parted company, the gullwing and I, when she was sold in 1961.

N782 ended her career a few years later when her new owner tried to use the aircraft as a mosquito sprayer near McGrath. The plane crashed and burned after a steep turn at the end of the runway.

As a fitting tribute, and with permission from Sig Olson, here is the poem he wrote recounting the many trials and tribulations we had with N782.

"ODE TO N-782"

The Gullwing is my aircraft,
*   I shall not rest;*
It flyeth me above the tundra
*   And leadeth me amongst mighty mountains;*
It maketh me to lie down after each flight
*   To recover my strength.*
*   It scareth my soul.*

Verily, thou taxieth like a lumber wagon,
*   Thou lovest the ground*
And no airstrip is too long;
*   Thine airspeed riseth but slowly;*
The end of the runway approacheth rapidly.
*   Yea, though I near the valley of the*
*   Shadow of Death,*
Thou art airborne! My sweat runneth over
*   But thy manifold pressure and tach needle*
They comfort me. I shall fear no evil!

Thou flyeth for hours and my bladder overfloweth,
*   For I dare not land short of a 3000 foot*
*   airfield.*

Alas! Thou preparest an emergency before me
*   In the presence of mine passengers:*
Thy prop seals giveth out
*   And thou annointest my windshield with oil;*
Thy governor refuseth to function
*   And I getteth a mere 1400 RPM from thee*
Thine oil pressure droppeth
*   And again my sweat runneth over.*
I calleth on the radio and receiveth no sympathy;
*   Smoke filleth thy cockpit and I cannot see —*
*   Thy smell overpowereth.*
Surely goodness and mercy hath deserted me forever.

I fighteth to maintain altitude,
*   I turneth thee back to Fairbanks International;*
At least thy rods and mains, they comfort;
*   Thou never stoppeth completely.*
But I forgetteth thy gas tanks and lo!
*   Thou hast stopped completely!*
My heart leapeth, my throat suddenly parcheth,

*   My hand flyeth to my left knee to switch tanks,*
Alas, thou art no Pacer!
*   Thy prop barely turneth over;*
Ah, Thy switch before my very eyes —
*   38 gallons more for thy gulping cylinders.*

Thy flaps commeth down, thy airspeed droppeth
    Anyway thy landing seemeth normal;
I taxieth thee and the pushers pusheth thee;
    I leaneth thee out and thy engine stoppeth.
Surely I shall consign thee to Hutch*
    Forever!

Amen

**Hutch was the mechanic that worked on N782 in
Fairbanks.*

Chapter 5

Fish and Wildlife Service Wives

BEHIND EVERY SUCCESSFUL MAN stands a devoted woman, as the saying goes, and when applied to the Fish and Wildlife Service agents 30 years ago, the word devotion took on a special meaning. We were expected to be on call 24 hours a day, and there was no such thing as an 8-hour day, 40-hour week, overtime pay or compensatory days off. Extensive travel was required due to the vast size of the area we patrolled, so consequently our home life suffered greatly.

It was during one of these patrols in the spring of 1954 that I met Elsie Sommer at her dad's store. I was sealing beaver in Nulato when we first met. For some reason after that I seemed to have a reason to go into that village more frequently than any agent had in the past. The people began to realize that it wasn't because they were violating the regulations more than others, but that there was another attraction there for me. Since I had to overnight somewhere on that end of the district on long patrols, and because Mrs. Sommer occasionally put up boarders, and because she served excellent meals, and because she had an attractive daughter, common sense dictated that it was a good place to stay.

Elsie, who had been away to boarding school in Oregon as a youngster and in San Francisco during nurses training, had come back to Nulato to help her aging dad run the store. She had planned on returning to the states in about a year to pursue a career in nursing; however, as one of the nuns at the Catholic mission later stated, it became obvious as time passed that she wouldn't make it. It was also obvious that my bachelor days were coming to an end. This was confirmed when I borrowed a friend's

44

plane and flew to Nulato from Fairbanks, a distance of over 300 miles, to propose marriage.

I tried to be honest in telling her what our life would be like after we were married, but I look back now and wonder if I was truly honest with her in explaining how much traveling I would be doing — but then, love has a way of jumping over hurdles and not bringing them into complete focus.

The Fairbanks district where I worked after Elsie and I were married in 1954 encompassed the area from Big Delta in the east to Unalakleet on the Norton Sound coast and everything north to Point Barrow. There were four agents working the district with only Ray Wolford, the enforcement chief, and I doing the flying. The bulk of the flying was left to me, however, because Ray was required to do most of the administrative work. That kept me busy and away from home many nights.

In 1956 I was transferred to McGrath as agent in charge of a district encompassing the Kuskokwim and lower Yukon rivers. I worked alone for more than two years before another agent was hired as an assistant. Most of the patrol efforts to cover the district required up to two weeks of travel; however, on occasion I would be gone three weeks or more. I didn't realize how much I was away from home until my wife presented me with her tally of days on the road for one year, and it amounted to more than six months of traveling. All this time she was at home caring for our small children, the house, and the Fish and Wildlife Service office. Fortunately, she was strong and understanding, or our marriage would never have survived.

During our first year of marriage in Fairbanks she kept busy nursing until our first daughter was born, after which she was a full-time mother. In addition to putting up with my absence most of the time, she got out of bed with me at all hours of the night when I had to go out on calls. Most were in response to moose that had been crippled or killed on the highway. We had to go out and dispatch the animal if it was crippled and field dress the critter for distribution to the needy. You would be surprised how fast you can butcher a thousand pound animal when it's 50 and 60 degrees below zero. Other calls concerned violations in progress, which we responded to as quickly as possible. By the time I was up and ready to go, Elsie would always have a welcome cup of coffee and a thermos for me to take along.

Occasionally I would bring home an orphaned animal for

Elsie to care for until I could find it a home. Once it was a fox pup that had been smoked out of its den by some military men. They had been reported taking the animal to the N.C.O. club and feeding it beer to the amusement of patrons. They had their day in court, and we had a fox with a badly burned nose. Elsie named him Hoikle, and we kept him in a spare bedroom, where he slept all day and kept us awake all night with his puppy

antics. Later I released him at Minto Lake where Pete Shepherd, a young biologist, was doing a study of muskrats. The fox stayed around Pete's tent all summer enjoying handout food and acting more like a domestic dog than a wild animal. Before the project ended that fall I watched as Pete tried to teach him to hunt mice for his survival that winter. We often wondered what became of him, hoping that he lived to be a ripe old fox but knowing inside that he probably became the victim of the first steel trap he came across.

We moved to McGrath in August of 1956. After getting established in a government log house built two years earlier, I departed for my first tour of the district. I had instructed Elsie on the use of the radio in the office in the front of our home. She had been reluctant to become a part of the Fish and Wildlife Service communications system until I told her I would need her to track my whereabouts by monitoring my flights. She finally agreed to talk to me only. However, it wasn't long before she became very adept at radio procedures and kept a log of all planes that were on patrols in remote areas. We kept the radio on day and night, and she assisted many pilots during off hours when the regular offices were closed.

On this, her first solo run, I advised her that I would call only when I was landing or departing because she already knew my itinerary. I followed the Kuskokwim River, stopping at each village to introduce myself, and ended up at the Aniak Roadhouse for the night. I beached the plane along the river front. Sometime before morning a big wind came up forcing me to spend a good deal of time tying off the Cessna 180's lines. Eighty mile per hour gusts threatened to flip the plane until I pumped water into the floats to partially submerge them. The extra weight may have saved the aircraft.

When the wind subsided the following day I pumped out the floats and took off in the direction of Bethel. I contacted Elsie and told her of my problems and plans. Her response was that maybe I had better consider returning home because the same wind hit McGrath, too, and half our metal roofing had blown off! I did a 180 degree turn and proceeded back upriver.

At McGrath I assessed the damage and radioed in an order for 30 sheets of roofing, which arrived the next day. The roof was repaired in short order.

I was more than upset with my spunky wife, who was 6 months pregnant with our second child, when I learned of her attempts to save the roof. Disregarding her condition, she ran after each piece of roofing that blew off toward the river only 90 feet away. Each time she picked up a 2-by-12-foot sheet she nearly went into the river herself, nevermind the continuous danger of being hit by other sheets. Luckily, a neighbor came along, grabbed a ladder, hammer and nails and saved the remaining roofing.

After all that I couldn't tell her that her troubles were for naught as none of the sheets she saved could be used again. Thankful she wasn't hurt, I asked her not to jeopardize herself again while I was gone. She shrugged and said you do what you have to do at the time and worry about it afterwards. I appreciated her all the more, but I could see I would be concerned each time I traveled.

The humorous part of the wind-and-roof episode occurred while she was calling on the radio, hoping I was on the air so she could advise me of the problem. The assistant aircraft supervisor in Anchorage, Tom Wardleigh, came on to give a bit of sage advice. "Just remember, Elsie, when you go out there in the wind, keep a cool head!" Pearls of wisdom in a time of crisis are always appreciated.

We spent Thanksgiving that year in Fairbanks waiting for the birth of our second daughter. It was extremely cold on December 10, the day we were to return, and Northern Consolidated Airways was having difficulties getting the DC-3 aircraft heated and ready for the run to McGrath. We were supposed to depart at 8 a.m. but did not take off until after 1 p.m. Because there was no phone at the home where we were staying, I was kept busy running back and forth to the neighbor's to get the actual time of departure. I frostbit my ears and nose in the process, but finally, we managed to get to the airport at the required time with Renee' our one year old and Michelle our newborn. Outside it was -40's, but the cabin was like a blast furnace from a Herman Nelson gas heater. Once the doors were shut and the engines started, however, it cooled off noticeably and remained quite chilly until the engine heaters kicked in.

A stop was required at Lake Minchumina, and the U.S. marshal from Bethel and I unloaded the mail and freight while the pilot kept one engine running. Two military passengers were dropped off at the Tatalina Radar Site, 15 miles from McGrath. This too was accomplished with one engine running. Finally, we arrived in McGrath at 5 p.m. with temperatures in the -50's. "Welcome back," a few hearty souls were shouting as we came down the steps of the plane with our new baby wrapped in blankets like a cocoon. We didn't stop to chat but rushed home only to find another dilemma — a house full of oil soot.

Prior to our departure for Fairbanks we had installed a new forced hot-air furnace to replace the old oilpot floor heater. The old heater and an oil stove were the only heat in the big two-story house, and after much pleading, the powers that be had finally come through with money for a properly designed furnace. When installed, it worked like a charm, blowing heated air throughout the house, and we were most anxious to enjoy the new system on our return. The week after we left, however, the hot water coil in the stove burst while our house-sitter, Harley King, was out for the evening. This in turn blew out the oven door, and soot, water and oil flowed through the kitchen and living room and down into the basement. When Harley returned he said he didn't know whether to lay down and cry or close the door and leave forever. Instead he hired a woman to help him, and together they mopped up the biggest part of the mess.

Don't try to clean up oil soot! You can't wipe it or sweep it. It just blows away or smears. The only thing that will remove it is a vacuum cleaner, and vacuum I did each time the hot air shut off and the soot settled. Then it was a complete washing of the ceiling and walls in the kitchen before calling it a night. The next day, Elsie pitched in and together we got most of it cleaned up; Renee' meanwhile playing on the floor, ended up looking like a garage mechanic, which didn't help.

Elsie never complained, but I knew that inside she had many reservations about this new life I led her into. Now we can look back and laugh about it all, and the children love the story of mother and the soot. I like to remind Michelle of how inconsiderate she was choosing that cold December to come into the world and how it had cost me a frostbitten nose and ears that peeled like onions for weeks afterwards.

The story Elsie likes to tell the most about her McGrath adventures involves the year that I appointed her the local beaver tagging officer. That particular year no one was available in town to tag beaver while I was traveling, so I persuaded Elsie to do her part for wildlife conservation and the "good ol'" Fish and Wildlife Service. There was only one problem; because she was my wife, I could not pay her the 10 cents per skin that the other tagging officers got. She reluctantly agreed, calling me a government cheapskate. Everytime I returned from a trip, she gave the details of the trappers who visited and laid their beaver skins on our living room floor to be tagged. The pungent odor wasn't offensive, but it was different and lingered for many hours after the greasy hides were taken away. Then, too, the trappers always arrived at the most inopportune times, such as when Elsie was feeding the baby or when dinner was being served. I kept telling her how important she was, what a good job she was doing, and how she was accomplishing something that only a few other privileged people in the world were authorized to do. Someday she would be able to keep audiences spellbound with her stories! All well and good she would say, but if I'm so important, why don't you pay me, and by the way, the total is now $26.50. All I could say was that someday I would reward her. When she became pregnant again, she advised me that she could do without my rewards!

In July we had a visit from Regional Director Clarence Rhode and several other chiefs who together were flying around inspecting the districts. They had dinner with us and stayed overnight. This was another of Elsie's McGrath duties — entertaining visiting dignitaries and coworkers. This she did with grace and diplomacy, never complaining. During dinner, however, she mentioned the beaver tagging operation and her cheap husband. I replied that it was unfair, but I had been informed that I could not pay my spouse on a government check. Clarence looked up and said, "Sure you can, and I so authorize it; pay Mrs. Tremblay." My mouth dropped, and then I sheepishly said that the books were closed for the fiscal year. There was no way of paying an obligation of the past year from this year's funds. The looks I got from Elsie said it all: I was in a world of hurt for $26.50. I've heard about it ever since and have paid my pound of flesh many times over for my indiscretion. It did no good to tell her I was only following the orders of the fiscal officer in Juneau. The chief said she should have been paid and that was good enough for her. Oh well, her other rewards have been many, and after three more children she agrees that it was worth it. Our six children also agree, and we can talk and laugh about the Fish and Wildlife days and the $26.50 that Dad still owes Ma.

All of the older Fish and Wildlife Service wives have their tales of what it was like in the pre-statehood days and of the many hardships they suffered while the men were out managing and protecting Alaska's wildlife, which at times seemed more important than the families. These women were truly the unsung heros of the Fish and Wildlife Service and unfortunately, they were never officially recognized. Without their patience and understanding we would never have been able to accomplish our missions. Alaska's wildlife owes them a great tribute. Those of us who are indebted to our dedicated wives will never forget. A few old-timers in the villages still remember — whenever Elsie returns to her village of Nulato, the older men still call her Mrs. Game Warden.■

Chapter 6

The Swallow and The Pacer

M OST PILOTS ARE AWARE or should be aware that birds and airplanes do not mix well. This not only includes birds that fly into the path of aircraft or get digested by jet engines, but also those that build nests in the engine nacelles or other convenient openings of parked planes. Woe be to the pilot who leaves his craft tied down for a few days when swallows are busy building their homes and does not check all openings for obstructions before taking off. He can be the victim of an overheated engine because his oil cooler is plugged by a tightly woven bunch of grass, twigs, twine, feathers and whatnot.

There are times, however, when even with the best pre-flight examination of the plane these feathered friends can get you in trouble, especially if you've been careless during previous flights. Such was the case in 1953 when a swallow almost caused the destruction of Fish and Wildlife Service Piper Pacer N702.

Several of these aiplanes were purchased in 1952 as patrol aircraft. They had already been proven as good bush planes easily adapted to wheels, skis and floats. Although built as a four-place plane, they were small, and most of the time we used them to haul only the pilot, another agent, and gear. "Gear" in winter was of a plumber's firepot, a can for draining oil, an engine cover, wing covers, sleeping bags, emergency equipment, snowshoes, heavy parkas, mitts and footgear. With all this stuffed in the back, there was no room for additional passengers.

When not flown for patrol the planes were used for game counts, waterfowl transects, tranporting staff and hauling freight. For game counts and personnel flights, the back seat was installed and three average-size passengers could be squeezed in. The

Pacers served us well until they were replaced in 1956 with the bigger and more efficient Cessna 180's.

After getting checked out as a Fish and Wildlife Service agent/pilot in January 1953, I assumed the biggest share of the flying responsibilities for the Fairbanks district. This included trapline patrols, beaver sealing trips, initiating the first waterfowl counts in the Interior, and responding to complaints in the villages. One such complaint was sent in by a teacher from the village of Venetie. He complained that too many moose had been killed and requested our presence in the village. Jim King and I responded on July 22.

The teacher met us at the small airstrip behind the village and briefed us on his concerns. While he had no problem with a moose being killed out of season by the Natives when there was a need for food, he was disturbed by the numerous hunting trips that were being made up river since breakup. On each trip several moose were killed. The hunters built a boat frame from willow or spruce poles, stretched the hide over it for a cover, and stacked the meat inside. The boat was then floated to the village. Additionally, there was a brush barricade that extended to a large lake located several miles north of the village. This fence had been built years earlier, probably prior to the use of rifles, to force moose and caribou through narrow openings where snares were concealed. From what we are able to learn these snares were made from braided spruce roots and were very strong. It was an ingenious way of taking game and worked quite well in the natural crossing between the village and the lake. While it was a necessary way of obtaining meat at one time, it was not needed in this day and age. However, according to the teacher, some of the villagers were still setting snares made of steel cable. He knew it was illegal to use snares for game animals, so he cut loose several moose he had found caught and thrashing around. We walked out the fence line and removed several snares and took pictures of two places where moose had been taken. The ground was torn up considerably indicating the animals had died a slow, agonizing death.

Back at the village we held a meeting with the few men that were in town. No one admitted any knowledge of the snares. It must involve several men hunting up river they said. When questioned about the number of moose being taken, they were just as vague. The teacher would not involve himself, and there was little we could do without witnesses or evidence. They agreed there was little need to continue hunting, and we emphasized our plans to make unannounced visits during the closed seasons. They said they understood and would advise other hunters.

When we left we flew up the East Chandalar River and located several boats that appeared to be the hunters we were told about. There was no gravel bar in the vicinity suitable for landing, so we headed back toward Fort Yukon for fuel after the engine sputtered. Looking around wasn't comforting because we were just coming out of the mountains and the terrain below did not look promising for a forced landing. Not to worry, however, because the engine picked up again and didn't miss a beat the rest of the way to the Fort Yukon airstrip. We shrugged it off and decided it must have been some water that was in the fuel and passed through the carburetor.

After refueling and draining the sumps thoroughly we continued on to Fairbanks. It was a beautiful clear day and the flight was smooth as we headed on a direct course that took us over the White Mountains toward the Tanana Valley. Then it happened again as we crossed Beaver Creek, a slight hesitation in the engine followed by purring all the way to Fairbanks. This time we suspected a little carburetor ice and shrugged it off again.

The next day was Friday, and we were in the office filing our reports and writing up an account of the patrol. Bob Scott, one of the game biologists, asked about the Pacer, indicating he was planning to use it the next day to make a caribou survey of the 40-mile country. I told him about the way the engine had acted and suggested he might want to have it checked by one of the mechanics before taking it out.

Saturday morning Ray Woolford received a call from a radio operator stating that Bob Scott had aircraft problems in Piper Pacer N702 and had made a forced landing at Caribou Creek. This was a mining strip on the headwaters of the Salcha River, about 65 miles from Fairbanks. Fortunately, we were able to locate a mechanic and departed about noon in the Gullwing Stinson to find out what the problem was. On the way up I briefed the mechanic about the way the engine in the Pacer had acted on our last trip, and he strongly suspected dirt was in the fuel system.

After landing, the mechanic questioned Bob about the engine. It had sputtered a few times after about an hour of flying and then lost power. Bob could not get more than about 1,400 RPM out of it no matter what he did, so he chose to land at Caribou which, fortunately, was near — a real piece of luck because landing strips are few and far between in that part of the country.

First thing the mechanic pulled the fuel strainer, and lo and behold it was full of feathers. Each time he drained the sump more downy feathers flushed out. He kept draining the sump until it appeared the system was cleared out, then he started the engine. It ran without any problem so Bob flew it back to Fairbanks while we followed with the Stinson in the event another problem occurred. The return trip was uneventful and N702 was tied down next to Fairbanks Aircraft Service for a complete going over on Monday. Before leaving we checked the fuel strainer again. More feathers!

Monday afternoon I went over to the shop to see how work was progressing on the Pacer. The entire fuel system had to be flushed out and mechanics were removing the empty fuel tank from the right wing. After it was lifted from its recess the tank was taken to a sink for cleaning. Something was rattling inside so the mechanic held it upside down and shook it until the object fell out. I picked up the culprit that had caused all the problems and sure enough, it was the remains of a small bird with most of its feathers missing. Now that was a head scratcher — how did he get into the fuel tank?

I took it back to the office and from the remaining feathers on the wing and tail we identified it as a swallow. Then we started pondering the mystery of why a swallow would be in a gas tank. The first thought was sabotage. Somebody at Venetie could have stuck the bird in the gas tank while we were walking to the moose fence, or it could have happened at Fort Yukon where we had stopped for fuel and lunch enroute to Venetie. We knew we weren't popular with many of the villagers because we had filed complaints against several of the trappers for illegal trapping the year before. We had our doubts that they were responsible, however, because they had never been vindictive; but then, times were changing.

We pondered the mystery for quite awhile, coming up with many possibilities, and then I remembered. In early June I had used the plane to fly waterfowl counts of the Kuskokwim valley. Dr. John Buckley and Dr. Brina Kessel were the observers and did the tallying while I flew the lines drawn on the map at exactly 100 feet altitude. (These first transects were most interesting because they had been selected randomly by biologists in Washington, D.C. They were so random that they went up and down mountains, across valleys and at times even over wetlands where ducks and geese were found. The maps were changed the next season with the transects transversing true waterfowl habitat. The revised transects have been used every year since and give an accurate picture of population trends of waterfowl production in Alaska. This year, however, we were doing the pioneer work and obviously mapping where the ducks were not. Negative information at times is as important as positive information I'm told.)

During the several nights we spent at McGrath John and Brina helped with the servicing and care of the plane. On June 4, according to my field diary, we left McGrath to run transects to Lake Minchumina. Prior to departure we topped off the gas tanks, and I paid our fuel bill at the Northern Commercial Company while my passengers finished getting the plane ready. We spent the night at Lake Minchumina and planned an early departure to complete the counts and return to Fairbanks. As we secured the aircraft I noticed a missing gas cap on the right wing and I chastised myself for not doing another pre-flight after returning from paying the gas bill. Someone forgot to put the gas cap back on and I didn't catch it. To make matters worse I could not locate anything to replace the cap at the airport maintenance facilities, so I decided to tie a piece of canvas over it for the night. When I got back to the plane several swallows were hovering over the fuselage and I made a mental note to give it a thorough looking over in the morning. I love birds. However, I didn't plan on making like a flying hotel and packing a nest back to Fairbanks. We spent the night at my old trapping cabin and I took the opportunity to make a few necessary repairs to the roof.

After a hasty breakfast I closed the cabin, and we took our gear back to the aircraft. I found no evidence of nesting. Everything else checked out okay except for the gas cap and that would have to wait until we got back. The rest of the trip was uneventful and I thought no more about swallows until we looked at this carcass on the desk.

I relayed the series of events that occurred at Lake Minchumina to the group that was assembled in the office. We all agreed that the swallow must have been looking over the open gas tank as a possible building site, became asphyxiated and spiraled in. That was over a month earlier and it had taken that long for the feathers to dislodge themselves from the carcass and travel through the fuel system. When I started thinking of all the forlorn country we had flown over with the bird in the tank I decided we were very fortunate not to have spiraled in ourselves. Like oil and water, birds and planes don't mix, and pilots must avoid them at all costs.

I've investigated many instances of inflight damage to planes from bird strikes, including one in which a hawk went through the windshield of a Supercub. Additionally, I've worked with airport managers trying to solve problems of keeping birds away from runways and in the process looked at several jet engines that were severly damaged from ingesting birds. In most of these accidents the plane was forced to land, but I've never heard again of any aircraft that was downed because of a bird in the gas tank.

Chapter 7

The Quiet Men

A MAN OF VERY FEW WORDS, and even those I found hard to hear," said the English ecologist F. Fraser Darling of Dave Spencer in his book *Pelican in the Wilderness.* I can't think of a better description of the U.S. Fish & Wildlife Service pilot/biologist in charge of the Kenai and Nunivak refuges. Dave is one of those rare persons you meet who has so many good qualities it is difficult to pick the most outstanding. He's an excellent pilot (World War II vintage), biologist, administrator, wildlife expert, outdoorsman and all-round great guy. The recipient of many conservation awards, he became the chief of the Alaska refuge system, and all who worked for or with him respected his resourcefulness and devotion to Alaska's wildlife problems. While at McGrath it was my good fortune to work with Dave and assist with the annual musk-ox count on Nunivak Island.

The island is located about 25 miles off the coast from near the mouth of the Kuskokwim River. Mekoryuk is the one village on the island. When I worked in the area the Eskimo residents were dependent on a hunting and fishing economy supplemented by seasonal work for the Bureau of Indian Affairs' reindeer program. Today the villagers own the reindeer and guide musk-ox hunters. They also trap foxes and carve walrus ivory.

Thirty-one musk-ox, originally obtained from Greenland, were introduced to Nunivak Island in 1935 and 1936 as a preliminary step in re-establishing them throughout their former range in Alaska. They once roamed the entire Arctic Slope, but the last known indigenous animals were killed by Eskimos near

Barrow about 1850-60. Nunivak Island was selected as the location to develop this herd since it was relatively accessible, free from predators and permitted confinement on a large area of good habitat. It was designated a National Wildlife Refuge by Congress.

Several counts of the animals were made by U.S. Fish and Wildlife Service personnel on foot and by dog team in 1942, 1947, and 1948. Aerial surveys were started by Dave Spencer in 1949, and they have continued since. Dave used a Grumman Widgeon at first, which is a smaller version of the Grumman Goose amphibian aircraft used so extensively by the U.S. Fish & Wildlife Service in Alaska. Later, in 1958, we started using the Cessna 180 because it was capable of slower flight and made a better survey plane. Today there are six well-established musk-ox herds on the Alaska mainland, all resulting from transplants from Nunivak. In addition, there are 500 to 600 musk-ox on Nunivak Island. Transplants continue and a number of both bulls and cows are annually killed by permit-holding hunters. Otherwise the herd would outgrow its range.

One very noticeable characteristic of Nunivak musk-ox is their low mortality rate. When I was involved there in the 1950s most of the dead animals were found by the Natives in their travels while trapping, hunting, fishing or herding reindeer. The locations of the carcasses were noted and always forwarded to Dave by mail. Any heads recovered were stored until Dave arrived, at which time the Eskimo finders were paid $5.00 for their services.

The skeletons of these deceased musk-ox were in demand at the time by museums. The bones were studied by curators and assembled for use by biology students and the interested public. With this in mind, Dave kept track of dead animals and after a year or more of exposure the bones would be well bleached by the weather. Marked on the map were those accessible for collection during the once-a-year survey.

One such carcass was marked on Dave's map in 1956, just a few miles up a drainage stream that emptied into Nash Harbor. The terrain sloped gently upward from the shallow bay into a series of grass benches. The skeleton was on top of one of these benches and had been checked by several parties of Eskimos during the spring of 1957. They attested to the fact that the bones were dry and could be easily picked up, so Dave suggested we make the collection during the survey in July.

Dave met me in Bethel on July 12. I had spent several days there distributing hunting and fishing licenses and discussing mutual enforcement problems with Deputy U.S. Marshal George Guilsher. Bethel was not my favorite place, and as the Widgeon lifted off the river, I looked back at the village and had no problem saying goodbye.

We landed in the harbor at Mekoryuk, put the gear down and taxied down the beach. As usual, most of the inhabitants walked down to greet us and help pack gear to our cabin. These were a happy people, always willing to lend a hand.

Later in the afternoon, a resident brought us a musk-ox

skull that he had found some months earlier. He was rewarded with Dave's $5.00. These Eskimos protected the musk-ox as their own, and Dave took the opportunity to ask who was familiar with the location of the musk-ox carcass behind Nash Harbor. A young hunter had been to the place several times and could guide us there. We would go the next day.

According to my field diary, we departed Mekoryuk at 8:45 the next morning. Aboard were two Swedish scientists researching Arctic flora, the young Eskimo guide, Dave and I. We circled the grass-covered bench where Dave had seen the carcass the year before and counted three creeks we would have to cross to get there. Because of high grass, we were unable to see the musk-ox remains from the air. We landed in the harbor and were beached at 9:05. Each of us grabbed a packsack and headed up the right side of the narrow river running into the bay. It was a beautiful day for an outing, and Dave set a brisk pace up the gradual incline.

After crossing the three small creeks flowing into the main river, we climbed up to the top of the hill, and found it flat as a tabletop stretching westward several miles toward the coast. We began walking five abreast in a westward direction searching for the bone pile. The bones were well hidden in the deep grass. We walked back and forth, east to west, then west to east, working our way along the bench in one-half-mile swaths. There wasn't much in the way of conversation; rather, we all seemed to be enjoying our own thoughts and gazing at the scenery in all directions.

Sometime around 12:30 p.m. Dave called a halt for lunch. One of the Swedish scientists, an expert on lichens had collected a few different samples, so at least her morning had been profitable. She produced some excellent cheese from her packsack to share as she explained some of the differences among plants. Dave, in his usual manner, said very little and the guide had not talked since departing Mekoryuk that morning.

We finished lunch and were basking in the sunshine when Dave said to the Eskimo, "I thought you knew where this musk-ox carcass was?" The Native replied, "No, I don't know where this one is, but there's one over there," and pointed to the next bench over.

We looked at one another in disbelief, picked up our packs and started out in the direction he had pointed. When we arrived on top of the next ridge our guide walked through the grass for about 300 feet and directed us to the musk-ox remains in just a few minutes. Dave shrugged and started dividing up the bones for each of us to pack.

As we started back to the plane, I thought to myself that I had finally met a person more quiet than silent Dave. The young Eskimo had been willing to go along on our trip to locate a dead musk-ox that he had seen several times while herding reindeer. Dave was relying on him to get us to the exact location. Knowing the approximate position of the animal, Dave had led the way thinking that our Native friend would take over as we approached the area. When we arrived on location, the Native assumed we were looking for a different animal and went along with the hunt without question until Dave finally requested his help hours later.

We arrived back at Mekoryuk at 2:30 p.m. and spent the remainder of the afternoon packing the bones for shipment to the National Museum. Feeling that I should test the ability of the specialists who would be putting the skeleton together, I threw in several reindeer bones for good measure.

Later that evening I asked Dave what he thought of our Native guide. Silent Dave answered, "He doesn't say much, does he!"

Chapter 8

Beaver

THE BEST EXAMPLE OF good wildlife management and law enforcement working together as a team has to be the reestablishment of beaver populations in Alaska. The largest member of the rodent family was heavily killed for his valuable fur and in the early 1900s was brought to near extinction from over-harvest and poor hunting techniques.

No animal played a bigger part in the history of North America than the beaver. Fur trappers and fur companies, such as the Hudson's Bay Company, pushed across the continent seeking beaver pelts, laying the foundation for future settlements from coast to coast. For years European hat makers used only beaver fur for felting material in Europe, and thousands of pelts were shipped to this market annually in the 18th century.

The famous Hudson's Bay Company extended its fur trade routes as far west as Fort Yukon in Alaska. Trade goods were transported from England to Montreal by ship, then in canoes and on the backs of voyageurs across Canada to the confluence of the Porcupine and Yukon Rivers. It took several seasons for the goods to arrive and the same amount of time for the beaver skins to travel east and reach the warehouses of investors.

It was not the steel trap that caused the over-harvest of this fur bearer, but rather it was the rifle. Shooting swimming animals after the winter ice melted off lakes and rivers was the easiest and most common way to harvest the beaver. It was also the most wasteful. Most trappers spent the spring months in canoes shooting beaver and muskrats. After spending six months living under the ice and snow both animals became tame following breakup. The hunter had only to paddle around the lakes and streams at his leisure watching for the telltale Vs in the water which marked the swimming animals. A well placed bullet did the rest.

Unfortunately, not all bullets were well placed, and therein was the problem. If the beaver was not killed outright before he expelled the air in his lungs he would sink and was lost to the marksman. Early trappers that I talked with admitted that losing three out of five beaver shot was not uncommon. It was this method that was the demise of the beaver, and by the 1920s the population was at an all time low.

The Alaska Game Law of January 13, 1925, provided the basis for wildlife management in Alaska. It set up a game commission of five appointed members, one from each of the four judicial districts and the fifth from the Bureau of Biological Survey (later to become the U.S. Fish & Wildlife Service). The commission had the power to employ game wardens for enforcement of the act and set the seasons and bag limits for the taking of game, fish and fur animals. It set up provisions for licenses, permits and a record keeping system for recording the numbers of game taken. It was under this authority that the commission authorized a system for marking legally taken beaver skins before they could be sold.

The first action taken to stop the excessive killing of beaver was to close the season completely. The 1925 regulations stated: Beaver and marten — No open season, may not be taken at any time. (There was also a concern for marten which were heavily trapped, and later in 1929 a limit of 10 was imposed on this animal.) For the next three years the season was open for the month of May with a limit of 20. Shooting with a rifle was permitted, but not by shotgun.The seasons for 1929-31 were entirely closed. The season opened again in 1932 in the upper Tanana and Yukon River watersheds from January 1 through March 31 with a limit of 10. Also introduced that year was a new provision under the methods of taking which read, "Beaver may be taken only by the use of steel traps, but such traps shall not be placed within 25 feet of any beaver house or den. No beaver may be taken by or with the aid of a rifle or shotgun or other firearm." In 1933-34, the season opened with a limit of 15. It closed again in 1935; however, for the 1936-37 season the commission changed the methods of taking again to allow the use of rifles.

When the season opened again in 1937-38, the limit was set at 10 where it remained until 1954 when the numbers of beaver started increasing again.

In 1940-41 the commission took another big step. The seasons had been closed as needed in those districts where the populations remained low without the desired results. The commissioners were aware that shooting was the problem; however, there was considerable pressure by the trappers to continue that method of harvest, so they wisely chose another course of action. They limited the taking of beaver to the early spring months while the lakes and rivers were still frozen. This was the most effective measure taken because it excluded shooting completely and forced trappers to learn to trap beaver under the ice. The season opened in February and closed on March 31, except for a few areas that closed on April 10. With the rifle eliminated and a limit of 10 beaver enforced by the use of an intensive sealing program, the animal made a spectacular recovery during the next 15 years.

The sealing regulation stated that no skins of beavers, whether taken within or without the Territory, could be exported from the Territory until the same had received a commission-prescribed seal.

My own experiences with the beaver program were both interesting and rewarding. Traveling to the different Native villages during and after the beaver trapping season to seal the skins was the highlight of the year's activities. As the spring days became longer and warmer, flying was more enjoyable, people on the traplines became more active, and there was a general feeling of accomplishment by everyone after the short, cold days of winter in Interior Alaska. When the trapping season ended on March 31, people congregated in the villages for a time of holiday. Each village had its rendezvous sporting dog team and snowshoe races. In the evening there were dances to enjoy when we overnighted.

Prior to the season we hired a tagging officer in each village. This was someone who had time to tag skins brought in by the trapper, usually a postmaster or teacher. They were paid 10¢ per skin, which could amount to $100-$150 a season.

There were two ways for a trapper to legalize his beaver skins. In either case an affidavit had to be completed stating his name, address, license number, if he were non-Native, the number of skins being presented, and the location where they were trapped. If it was a tagging officer handling the skins he would fold the affidavit into an envelope, place a special string through one leg hole of the hide or hides and through a soft lead coupler, which was then pinched together with a serial numbered plier. The hide or hides (the trapper could tag them one at a time or all 10 together) was then legal to sell or transport within the Territory. Usually the trappers would tag their beaver and then sell them to the local trader. The trader would hold them for sealing, after which they would be shipped to one of the fur houses, most often the Seattle Fur Exchange, and sold at auction.

The seals we used were metal and similar to those used on railroad box cars. They were numbered in sequence with 100 to a bundle. One end had a locking device, and the other was perforated. The seal was looped through a leg hole, one to a skin, and slipped into the lock. Once the locking pin was in place, the seal could not be removed without breaking it. Each seal number was carefully recorded on the affidavit of the trapper taking the beaver, and at the end of the season the seal numbers were listed on a form with the trapper's name. This form plus the affidavits were sent to Juneau for filing; thus, there was a complete record of each beaver taken by date, locality, and trapper.

We started our rounds through the district sealing skins once they started piling up at trading posts. We also patrolled traplines and sealed skins at trappers' camps. This was an added service to the trappers and helped to slow down the take of over-limits furs that could be sealed by family members or friends who had not been out trapping.

While I was working out of the Fairbanks office in the early 50s the biggest concentration of beaver was taken in the mid-Yukon and Koyukuk River watersheds. We usually operated from the village of Koyukuk, centrally located within this vast area. Local trader Domenic Vernetti usually bought more skins than any other trader in Alaska. We made the rounds of the villages every two weeks, weather permitting, sealing all the beaver the traders had purchased, enabling them to ship them to market.

It was not uncommon to walk into a trading post in late March and find several piles of tagged skins stacked along a wall five to six feet high. Whenever I looked at one of these piles, which represented the limits of 20 or more trappers, I thought about the fur trade of the 18th century in Canada. In those days the value of a six-foot musket was a pile of beaver hides stacked along an upright gun to the tip of the barrel. That's a lot of beaver, and was the result of a great deal of labor for a weapon of the lowest quality produced at that time.

Two of us would situate ourselves beside the pile with a box to write on. One opened envelopes and called out the number of skins tagged. The other counted out the number of seals and read off the first and last numbers. While these numbers were being recorded with the date of sealing, the seals were attached and a new pile of the sealed beaver started. The process could last anywhere from a few minutes to several hours depending on the number of hides. When completed, we moved on to another trading post (several of the larger villages had more than one store) and then continued on to another village.

While enroute to the different villages we would patrol traplines and check to assure that traps and snares were the legal distance (25 feet) from beaver houses. Those that were too close were pulled and the trapper contacted. If the violation warranted action, he would be taken before the closest U.S. commissioner. If he was found guilty, the usual fine was $50, and we flew him back to his home village.

On one patrol of the Andreafsky River in the lower Yukon country, I spotted a beaver house that had at least 30 different sets around it. Beaver were not plentiful in that area, and apparently several trappers were competing for the few animals available. Some snares were set at the legal distance while the remainder were set progressively closer to within a foot or two of the house. Obviously, as each trapper moved in to make a set he had to get closer than his competitor due to the limited space available. It reminded me of the Maginot Line, and I wondered how any beaver could swim anywhere in the vicinity without getting fouled in wire and steel. A dog team was approaching the small lake and I was able to land and make contact with the driver, a Native from Mountain Village. He became noncooperative when I introduced myself and immediately claimed he could not understand much English. This was an old ploy which had been used on me before, so I spoke slowly and used diagrams in the snow to explain my concern over the illegal sets. He kept nodding and shrugging until I paced out 25 feet and pointed out the snares that were set the legal distance and all those that were too close to the house. My patience was waning at his games of "me no understand" when it was obvious that he knew exactly what I was saying. Finally, I asked him very slowly which were his

sets. Without hesitation he walked over and picked out several that were the legal distance from the house. Now I could only shrug and think to myself, "What the heck — beat again." Then I asked him his name. His answer: Rusty Prunes. That did it. I told him to make sure he advised his friends about the 25 foot regulation as I pulled up all the illegal snares and left while I still had any sanity.

Later I stopped at Mountain Village and inquired about a man called Rusty Prunes and was told that indeed that was his name. Seems like years back when the Bureau of Indian Affairs was anxious to make sure all Natives had proper surnames, the trader at this village helped them pick out names of store goods; consequently, there are families of Beans, Coffees, and, of course, Prunes! My education was continuing by leaps and bounds.

While I was stationed at McGrath the majority of my work was with Natives, both Indian and Eskimo. In that capacity I likened my role to that of a referee. My main job was to enforce the game laws, which were designed to assure healthy populations while allowing the surplus to be harvested. Seasons and bag limits had to be monitored. However, there had to be some latitude and reasonableness applied when dealing with people who were completely dependant on fish and game as a food source. It was then that the role of referee came into play — to assure that all had a fair chance to take the available game without making serious inroads into the population stocks. In that capacity I often answered complaints from the villagers worried about others killing more than they needed. I kept a few of the letters that best illustrate the problems considered serious enough by villagers to write against some of their neighbors. The first was written from a Yukon village on December 8, 1957, (the beaver season did not open until February 1) and is copied verbatum, leaving out the names of the people involved.

Dear Sir:

I do not like to report such things against my neibers, but we all want to play fair with Government by fair hunting and by fair fishing we all do try best of our ability to do good and honest hunt and fishing. I have seen with my own eyes that the Beaver houses were smashed open and the beavers were killed on the spot by these 3 men [names omitted] and some of these men have dependent money from government, thats why I want a game warden to come here this instent to over look at there beaver catch now, and no waiting, I have seen 2 drying and 1 not dry'd yet and they were still active in smashing open the Beaver houses I have seen 2 Beaver houses been open'd by these 3 men some of these men get money from Government that is aid-dependent money — and they are not suposed to do this bad trick against us and many children who have no parents here and all over alaska — thats just like trying to destroy money for alaska neibers. If you ever come to [village name deleted] for this investigation please do not mention my name, as a reporter against these men — because I want you to ask me questions in personal, have your interpeter [name deleted] who is always at home — and all the councils know these men who are hunting Beavers at this, But one of the councils have told these

3 men to keep hunting right in front of my open eyes in one room house. This is it I want game warden here now with a looking in a house for fur-permit — now.

Another from a village up-river is quite lengthly and is quoted only in part.

Dear Mr. Tremblay:
Just a few lines that I feel is my duty to write you thinking you were still our game warden around this neck of the woods and know you would be able to catch some of the birds that set their traps right up against the beaver houses and those that chop into the houses. There were two brothers last year that trapped between 80 to 90 beaver last season. In fact when they returned they had their father and mother sign up a lot of beaver. He and his wife never left the village. I think they will in the near future start hauling the traps out and will have them all over the country same as last year. Ray I hate to report this to you but I think its my duty to do so. So kindly do not let anyone know that I wrote you this information. Let me know right away if you received this letter.
Yours truly,
[name withheld]

Several of these letters were received every season from different villages throughout the district. Most were from the older people who were genuinely concerned about wildlife because they had been dependent on fish and game for their livelihood before there were such things as government grants and welfare. They had known hunger and had no problem with game being taken out of season so long as it was needed and used. Sharing was also an important part of their culture and dividing up the spoils with those unable to go out was encouraged. What really caused problems, however, were the younger men who would not work and made illegal kills whenever they felt like it. Even then it took courage to turn in their own people, but they were concerned that overkilling would deplete the very wildlife that many depended on.

I followed up every complaint. Sometimes it was possible to catch the guilty parties and other times meetings were held with the village councils to get their cooperation in stopping the overkilling. Most of the time they pledged their help and were able to slowdown the needless slaying. The control of the village elders no longer exists today and unfortunately, this method of conservation is a thing of the past.

It was encouraging to see the beaver make a comeback through our enforcement efforts, education and good wildlife management practices. They now have expanded their range and are even a nuisance in some areas. I think everyone agrees that the rehabilitation of this animal in Alaska was a milestone in the annals of wildlife conservation.

Like everything else, just when you think your work is finished for the season, after traveling constantly to tag all the beaver in the district, you receive a letter like this:

Nicholai — Salmon River
April 10, 1959

To Alaska Game Commission
McGrath, Alaska

When you were at Nicholai on April 4th to tag Beavers you come to soon for me. I come leta that night with my Beaver skins so I don't get my Beaver skins tag yet and I got big family. Beaver price is bum this year I cant not pay air plane fare to McGrath and I will be in Salmon river and if you want to tag my beavers before brack up you just come to salmon river at the lake will be pretty good for few more days only.

[name withheld]
P.S. I cant spent Beaver money on air plane trip to you.

I made a special trip up to Salmon River and sealed all his beaver. That ended the 1959 season with close to 10,000 skins sealed in the McGrath District during the last year of territorial status. The newly created Alaska Department of Fish and Game took over control of all resident fish and game in 1960.

Chapter 9

More Beaver

THERE WERE OTHER FACETS of the beaver management program that were just as interesting and important as the sealing, tagging and enforcement efforts we conducted. One was the conservation essay contest held at the Fairbanks High School each winter and sponsored jointly by the school system, the U.S. Fish and Wildlife Service, and the Tanana Valley Sportsmen's Association. Each year an Alaskan wildlife conservation theme was chosen by a committee of the three groups and then presented to the senior class. Essays based on the theme had to be completed by students by February 1. The two winners (one girl and one boy) were rewarded with a three-day trip to villages on the Yukon and Koyukuk rivers to assist with the beaver sealing program.

The trip would begin on a Friday morning in early April with two planes. The students were accompanied by chaperones, usually teachers who had assisted with the contest. Expenses were paid by the Sportsmen's Association. We departed Fairbanks and flew direct to Ruby, sealed all the beaver on hand at the two trading posts and then went on to Galena and Nulato. After we sealed beaver at John Sommer's store in Nulato, we toured the village and the Catholic mission, the oldest in Alaska.

Nulato is the site of the most-inland Russian trading post built in the early 1800's. In February, 1851, English naval Lt. J.J. Barnard of the HMS Enterprise, which was anchored in Saint Michaels, was a guest of the Russians. Barnard was searching for information of the famed Franklin expedition lost in the Arctic several years previously. Lacking an understanding of Indian culture, Barnard sent for the chief of the Koyukuk tribe, but he did so without the proper diplomacy. The Koyukuk Indians killed the Russian messenger and his Native guide. They then proceeded to Nulato and killed most of the villagers who were congregated in several large underground houses for the night. The fort, which was about a mile away, was attacked next and several Russians were killed. The attackers were finally driven off, but not before Lieutenant Barnard and the Russian commander died from knife wounds. They are buried side by side behind the mission ground. Barnard's grave marker reads "Lieutenant J.J. Barnard of the HMS Enterprise killed February 16, 1851 by the Koyukuk savages."

At the end of this interesting tour of Alaska history we continued to Koyukuk to overnight. This was rendezvous time, and the small village overflowed with people. A potlatch and dance highlighted the evening festivities. The next morning we watched dog races and assisted in chopping out the village fish trap from its location on the river. The occasion was enjoyed by both the visitors and the villagers eager to share their friendship.

The Vernetties were great hosts and made the visit a rewarding experience for guests. Ella, an Athabaskan woman born and reared here, gave vivid accounts of Indian life and displayed her many artifacts of moose hide garments decorated with beautiful beadwork and porcupine quills, birch bark baskets, and bone tools. Her husband Domenic, an italian immigrant who had walked the Iditarod Trail in the early 1900's, cooked up scrumptious, not-to-be-forgotten meals. All in all, a very rewarding experience.

About noon we departed to tour Huslia, a village on the Koyukuk River, to take care of the skins at Jack Sackett's trading post. Jack, another old-timer and great story teller, would spin a few yarns of the early days to the delight of our visitors. Then it was off for Hughes where we spent the night with Mr. and Mrs. Les James. Here again, the rendezvous was in full swing with dog races and other events going on. In the evening there was a big dance that went on all night. The students always mixed in well and usually participated in every dance from the two-step to the jigs. It was never an energetic crew that arrived at the breakfast table Sunday morning in preparation for the trip home.

The trip back took us up the Koyukuk River to the village

of Allakakett to visit the Episcopal mission and to seal what few beaver might be on hand. There were seldom very many since most of the people were at Hughes. It was then on to Bettles for lunch and back to Fairbanks in the late afternoon.

The thank-you letters we received told it all — a great adventure, a historic trip back into time, a better understanding of Native culture and a deeper appreciation for wildlife conservation. Everyone benefited, and we had hopes of expanding the affair, but unfortunately, the legalities of government culpability in the event of an accident ended it.

With the build up of beaver populations came the age-old problem of man and animal trying to live together. In this case this animal's need for deep water to build a house with an underwater entrance was in question. It is well known that beaver accomplish this by building dams across streams which cause them to spread out and can play havoc with people living in the lowlands. The dams never seem big enough to these engineering marvels, and if a particular valley has enough good feed available, they will add to the dam's size, creating large ponds and lakes. This gives the beavers a place to build a home free from predators. However, as the flood plain spreads, it inundates roads, cultivated lands, and homes. It was not a case of who was there first, because man always won, but rather a case of "the beaver must go," which was not as easy as it sounded.

We had constant complaints from the Alaska Road Commission on highway culverts being plugged in areas of good beaver habitat. Plugged is a good word because the culvert would be so jammed with sticks, stones and mud that it would take one or two men hours with crowbars and axes to pull it apart. Then within one or two nights it would be plugged again — such is the tenacity of these animals. How to control the problem without killing off the animals (which seldom worked because beaver from other areas would move in if it was a good stream)? The solution: Heavy duty screen panels were fit into slots on both sides of the culvert. The beaver would build against the screen but one man could patrol the road system, pull a panel, and free the debris in a matter of minutes. Eventually the animals became discouraged and vacated the stream.

Another sticky problem was dams that flooded homestead roads and homes in the bottom lands. The owners wanted the dams lowered to control the water level, yet they did not want to hurt or lose the beaver because they enjoyed having the beaver as neighbors. Anyone who has worked with these animals realizes that you can blow holes in dams with dynamite to lower the water and the colony will have the damage repaired in one night. A meeting and another solution! Twenty foot lengths of four inch pipe were hauled to the affected areas. A notch was cut into the middle of the dam down to the level of the desired water table. One end of the pipe was layed into the slot so it just protruded out the back end of the structure. The other end was set into a cradle in the river bottom upstream from the dam. Upon confronting this situation the beaver would pack in the notch solid but could never figure out how to stop the flow of water. They always attacked the problem from the upstream side of the dam and since they could never locate the source of the leak with the pipe opening some 15 feet or more upstream, they gave up. This then kept water at a constant level, deep enough in most cases for their purpose and low enough so it did not flood the neighborhood. Everyone was happy and we were heroes.

In some areas the only solution was to trap the beaver alive and move them to another location. We soon found out that they had to be moved a considerable distance and into a different watershed or they would return. The trap used was made from a heavy-duty metal mesh and designed similiar to a suitcase. When opened, a trigger mechanism kept the trap from closing until the trigger depressed, which released a powerful spring assembly to close the two sides of the trap together. It was set layed out flat on the ground and baited with fresh birch or alder branches. The beaver walking over the mesh eventually set off the trigger and was immediately "suitcased" and ready for a truck ride to a new location.

On one occasion I had a trap set by a slough in the vicinity of several homeowners who were losing a number of good trees to some rogue beaver. I had picked up several animals and moved them without a problem until one morning I found a sprung trap. At first I suspected a person of tripping the trap, which happened occasionally, until I talked with one of the local residents. He told me that on the previous evening, he saw the biggest beaver ever approach the trap and hid himself to watch the encounter. After sniffing the surrounding area, the giant beaver walked onto the trigger. The trap was sprung, but the beaver was so big that instead of snapping shut around him, the trap catapulted him into the air over the bank and into the slough. The last the witness saw of him he was making like a racing boat with throttles wide open going downstream. We never did capture that rascal, and he continued to plague the neighborhood until some poor sport shot him. It was costly, though, as he had to pay a healthy fine for his indiscretion.

Quite often beaver would dam important salmon streams completely, stopping a run of fish from getting to the spawning grounds. When this occurred, it was, and still is, necessary to blow up the dam and keep it open until the run is complete. Then a follow-up is required to allow the smolt to swim downstream and complete the cycle.

It was during my first dam busting operation that I became well acquainted with Slim Moore. Slim, who died on April 3, 1982, at age 83, was one of Alaska's original and oldest registered hunting guides. He was licensed as a master guide, and for his dedication to guiding and his devotion to fair chase in the taking of game, he was the first recipient of the Simon-Waugh Award given by the Alaska Professional Hunter's Association. He spent some 50 years as a guide and trapper and was well known and respected for his commitment to wildlife conservation. His sharp wit and ability to relate past experiences and foster honesty in the taking of game endeared him to all conservationists and wildlife managers.

In the early 1950s Slim was operating a lodge located on the shores of Summit Lake on the Richardson Highway. The outlet of Summit Lake flows into Paxton Lake and then into the Gulkana River, which in turn meanders into the Copper River. The Copper River winds its way through the Alaska Coastal Range and empties into the Gulf of Alaska near the town of Cordova. This entire watershed plays host to enormous runs of spawning salmon and is vital to the survival of several species, especially the sockeye. Finding their way to the headwater lakes after traveling hundreds of miles of glacier silted waters is a miracle in itself for the fish. Being stopped by a beaver dam must be the ultimate frustration.

Such was the case with the outlet stream of Fish Lake which feeds into the river connecting Paxton and Summit lakes. In 1953 beaver built a large dam several hundred feet downstream from

Fish Lake causing it to rise several feet. The lake is about four miles long so the two-foot rise was significant in the volume of water being held back. Behind the dam were thousands of red salmon trying unsuccessfully to enter the lake to spawn along the shore line. The dam had to go and I was sent up with a Super Cub and a load of dynamite to do the job. As I gingerly loaded the ominous looking cardboard box of explosives I wondered "Why me?" I knew nothing about dynamite or how to use it. I was told to protect the caps carefully and not load them near the dynamite, for an inadvertent jar could cause the plane and me to disappear. The explosives were in the back beside a movie camera. I put the caps, carefully wrapped in cloth, inside my shirt. I was advised to talk with Slim Moore for advice since he had worked around mining camps and would have experience on the use of explosives.

I landed at Summit Lake with the float equipped cub, and Slim was right out to help me beach and tie down. Would he help with the project? "When do we start?"

"After lunch please," was my reply. I wanted to relax awhile away from the dynamite laden plane. It had been rough flying in the pass, and I had sat on the edge of my seat all the way there, as if a few more inches between the caps and the box would help. In my mind it did, and that's all that mattered because I had arrived safe and sound. (Years later I hauled over a ton of dynamite with a Grumman Goose from a lake in the Kenai Mountains to the town of Lawing for the Forest Service. Even though I was more comfortable about the flight, I had to admit that my landing was the smoothest ever and when the wheels first made contact with the gravel runway nary a pebble was disturbed. It's interesting how our senses get so finely tuned when we're apprehensive even though we can act so nonchalantly on the outside.)

Late in the afternoon I took off with Slim, who barely fit in the back seat with the box in his lap. He was in his usual jovial mood and kept joking about how we should make a pass over his competitor at Paxton Lodge so he could drop one stick down the chimney, just for sport.

Once on the ground Slim eyeballed the dam like a log driver searching out the key log to blast. Finally satisfied with the right location he took several sticks and taped them together onto a pole. As he made a slit into one stick and inserted a cap and fuse, I readied the movie camera. He waterproofed with grease and poked the gear into the dam. Once the fuse was lit we made a beeline to a prepicked spot where we could watch in safety.

I started the camera to capture the event on film for future PR work. Just before the big blast a female mallard swam into view, and I yelled to Slim, "Chase her away before she's hamburger."

He yelled back, "Forget it, friend — better her than me. It's too late now." Thirty seconds later it blew and although the mallard didn't suffer the fate of being minced, she made the dangdest catapulting takeoff I ever did see. It would have made a dandy movie sequence except that I jumped when the blast went off and all I got was a picture of the sky.

Once opened, the water began pouring through filling the stream bank full. Many unfortunate salmon were washed downriver a good distance before recovering and some got carried all the way to the mouth. What an unglorious ending to a super migration effort. Fortunately, several days later the creek stabilized and we watched hundreds of salmon making their way into the stream. I camped on location for about a week keeping the dam open until the major share of the run had passed through.

I went back to Summit Lake and had a long talk with Slim about the fate of this family of beaver. I had counted seven all told and felt they had to be removed. Slim indicated that it would be difficult to do during the open trapping season because of the snow depth. He agreed to give it a try if we issued him a permit to trap in November and December when he would be able to get to the lake on snowshoes. It was agreed, and I told him the necessary paper work would be issued in plenty of time. I reported back and told my supervisor that once we issued the permit we could forget about the beaver because it was just like the Mafia negotiating a contract — Slim the hit man would do the job.

I thought no more about the problem until one day in December when I got a call from Slim's wife saying he was in the hospital recuperating from an appendectomy. When I went up to visit I found him propped up in bed looking all tanned and ruddy against the white sheets and no indication that he had been through an operation. He was his jovial self as he gave me the details of the incident that put him in the hospital. Fortunately, his wife Margaret had been accompanying him on his jaunts up to Fish Lake to trap out the beaver. She was quite adept on snowshoes herself and often helped Slim with his traplines. That particular morning he hadn't felt up to snuff but not bad enough to stay home, so they put on the webs and plodded the four miles up the creek to the lake and checked the traps. They had one beaver and were proceeding back home when Slim was hit with a severe attack of abdominal pains. Somehow Margaret assisted him back to the road, although I don't know how because Slim was a big man. Once to the road she got out the pickup and drove him to Fairbanks. As Slim put it if Margaret hadn't been there he would have cashed his chips in right then and there on the trail. Then he grinned and said he got a ribbing from his doctor who claimed Slim's appendix was chock full of ptarmigan feathers. "He told me I should clean my birds before I eat them. Now ain't that a heck of a note to have to change my ways this late in life!"

Slim recovered and finished trapping out the family of beaver. The next year there was no dam for the fish to contend with and I had gained the lasting friendship of a great Alaskan. I was honored years later when he sponsored me for membership into the Pioneers of Alaska after I had fulfilled the 30 years residency requirement. All of this as a result of my continuing encounters with beaver.■

Chapter 10

Charlie Woods

CHARLIE WOODS WAS TYPICAL of many old timers who chose to live their senior years in the solitude of wilderness Alaska. Most of his breed refused to submit themselves to retirement homes. They sought no help from anyone, suffered the chronic aches of the aged in silence, and were content to live their last years in the peace and silence of the big woods.

Like many others, Charlie grew a garden in the summer, enduring the myriads of mosquitoes to produce a year's supply of vegetables. His eyes were failing so he was not always successful at moose hunting, but someone always managed to drop him off a piece of meat before freeze up. He had an old boat and motor that he used to make an annual 100-mile river trip to McGrath each summer for seeds, clothing, and staples. He only stayed a few days to visit a friend, cash his pension checks, gather up his mail and supplies, and head back again for another year.

In the summer of 1957, however, Charlie didn't show up in McGrath. No one was too concerned at first because there was never a specific date for his arrival. About August 20 several Indians from the village of Telida came to town with disturbing news. They always checked on Charlie when they traveled the north fork of the Kuskokwim River as his cabin was midway between their village and McGrath. They reported to U.S. Commissioner Pete Egrass that Charlie's boat was tied up in front of his cabin all loaded for a trip, but no one was around. They checked inside the cabin and noticed that the last day marked off on the calendar was August 10th and there was no recent signs of occupancy. They searched the area surrounding the cabin but found so sign of him anywhere. Now people were concerned.

Pete Egrass notified the Territorial Police at Fairbanks, and on August 21 Lt. Bill Trafton and Sgt. Emery Chapple arrived in McGrath to make an investigation. After talking with the local people who knew Charlie and getting all the information they could about him, they came to my office seeking assistance. Would I fly them to his cabin so they could conduct a search? This was no problem since the Cessna 180 was all gassed and ready to go. We departed after telling several of Charlie's friends that we would come back for them if help was needed.

The river in front of Charlie's cabin was long enough for a landing and subsequent takeoff, so after eyeballing it carefully for driftwood, I touched down and taxied up alongside his boat. We were able to tie up and use the boat as a float, which was a break since the river was quite swift with a steep, muddy bank, making it unsuitable for beaching. With the plane secure we began our search for some clue as to Charlie's whereabouts.

Everything was as the Indians had described. Charlie's boat was indeed ready for a trip — all equipped with gas and food. It was a large riverboat over 20 feet in length, which Charlie hauled out each year with block and tackle and launched in the summer using greased poles, ropes and pry bars. His camping gear was stored under a seat and his sleeping bag was in a waterproof box along with extra clothing. It appeared as if he had been ready for immediate departure.

In the cabin we looked at the calendar which had an X through each day through the 10th, a common way for people living alone to keep track of time. The dishes were clean and in place and everything pointed to the fact that he had been leaving for McGrath on the 11th when he met with some misfortune.

After searching the surrounding woods and trails without any success, we turned our attention to the river. We theorized that he had been loading the boat and had fallen into the river due to a slip or possibly a heart attack. We searched downstream, checking the driftwood piles in eddies for any sign of a body, all to no avail. So it was back to McGrath to make arrangements for closing up the cabin and storing his property. Lieutenant Trafton and Sergeant Chapple departed the next day for Fairbanks leaving the final details to Commissioner Egrass and me. Their report listed Charlie Woods as missing and an apparent victim of drowning. Everyone in McGrath accepted the theory and said it had been bound to happen someday.

Two days later on August 22, I took Commissioner Egrass and a McGrath resident back to the cabin. Together we made another effort to find Charlie's body, without success. We gathered up all his belongings and loaded them into the boat. After closing up the cabin the two men started downriver in the boat while I flew the Cessna back to McGrath. Charlie had disappeared, which was not an uncommon occurrence with the strong-willed loners who choose a hermit's existence over the confines of the settlements.

Every once in awhile during the next few months the subject of Charlie was brought up at a gathering or at one of the local pubs, and it always ended with the same question, "Wonder what really happened to him?" or, "Wonder how Charlie finally bought it?" The old timers accepted the passing of one of their group without a great deal of remorse — they had all lived full lives —

but they liked to know how the end had come. When they sat around reminiscing and telling stories on the ones who were gone, there was always a big void at the end if the person had just disappeared. It was always an unfinished story. It's the same with all of us; we like to bury our dead, and when they end up missing we can never be sure that they're truly gone. So the talk continued about Charlie throughout the winter months.

Then on March 4 an Indian from Nikolai sent a message to the commissioner. He had been trapping north of Charlie Woods' place and his trail passed behind the cabin. On a return trip he had found a hip boot that had been dragged out and left by animals on his dog team trail. A bone protruded from the end. He reported that he had not touched it, nor had he looked for any other remains.

The next day I flew Commissioner Egrass back to Charlie's place. We landed again on the river but this time on skis. The snow was deep so we strapped on snowshoes and started following the Native's dog team trail past the cabin. Sure enough, about three quarters of a mile behind the cabin there was the hip boot with a leg bone inside. The boot had been worn folded down and the bone was broken off just below the knee joint. The tracks around the area were made by wolves, and by backtracking the most used trail we located more human bones. Further examination produced a pelvis, ribs and a skull. We took pictures and tried to reconstruct what had happened, with little success due to the snow depth.

Two things were obvious: First, this had to be Charlie; and second, the wolves had nothing to do with his death. They had located the remains and dug them up, carrying some of the bones to other locations. We collected all the remains we could find (the second boot was never found), put them in a sack, and proceeded back to McGrath.

Several days later a coroner's inquest was held. Charlie Woods' remains with all the information gathered so far was presented to a local 6-man jury. Discovered during the inquest was a small caliber bullet hole in the skull just above the location of the right ear. The jury concluded that the cause of death was from a self-inflicted bullet wound. Before the book on Charlie was closed, however, the weapon needed to be located, if possible. When Lieutenant Trafton, Sergeant Chapple and I had made the inspection of Charlie's cabin the previous August we had found an empty box on one of the shelves that had contained a .22 caliber Harrington and Richardson automatic pistol. We had searched the cabin and the boat for the pistol without success. Now the pistol became an important part of the cause of death conclusion, and the jury requested that we go back after breakup and try to locate it.

Because I was involved in some long patrols that spring along the Arctic Coast to Point Barrow, the plane was not put on floats until the middle of June. Finally, on Sunday morning June 22, Commissioner Egrass and I went back to Charlie's homestead for the last time. We went back to where we had discovered the skeleton remains and searched the area. Sure enough, right where the bones had been was a rusted H&R pistol. Pete checked it very carefully and determined that it was fully loaded except for one empty round in the chamber.

Thus ended the "Saga of Charlie" except for the big question, "Why?" Why was his boat ready for the annual trip to McGrath? What was he doing back in the woods, and did he always carry the .22 pistol with him on his walks? Did he go back there to commit suicide?

Everyone familiar with the story had his or her ideas and theories. Most agreed, however, that Charlie was not planning suicide, but something had occurred that caused him to end his life unexpectedly. My theory follows simple logic. He went back into the woods to cut some poles for navigating the boat and met with some accident. It could have been a broken leg, a severe cut with an axe, or a stroke, or heart attack. Once incapacitated, he knew the consequences of lying seriously injured, alone, with no help forthcoming. He would have two choices, end it all, or lie there suffering until the end came. To a man in his late 80's the choice was simple, and he chose the quick and easy route.

Whatever the reason, he ended his life as many others living in seclusion have, but he was happy, lived the life he wanted and stayed until the end in the country that he loved. A time to live and a time to die. Charlie had picked the one place in the world he loved to do both, and on his own terms.￭

Chapter 11

Game Check
Stations

BEFORE THE HORDES OF PEOPLE arrived in Alaska it was always an interesting experience to work on the Steese Highway or 40-Mile Road during the hunting season. We usually set up game check stations, which consisted of trailers positioned at strategic locations, manned by both biologists and enforcement agents. All outgoing vehicles were stopped and hunters checked to assure they had taken legal animals. A great deal of good biological data was obtained by collecting and studying the game's lower jaws, organs, height and weight.

The check stations were open 24 hours a day. We took turns working with a biologist. An enforcement agent was on duty at all times to handle the traffic. On weekends several more would join the crew, and even so, it was not uncommon to have 30 or 40 cars backed up waiting to be checked.

When not at the check station we were busy patrolling the roads. Regulations required hunters to be at least a quarter mile off the road to take big game, and there were several major caribou crossings where regulations required a hunter to be at least five miles off the road side. These protected five-mile zones allowed the caribou to cross the highway unmolested and gave the non-hunter a place to observe the animals without fear of being shot. Additionally, the Alaska Game Law prohibited the taking of cows and calves of moose and caribou. This posed no problem with moose. However, it was a different story with caribou as both sexes have antlers. While management biologists did not agree with the law, there was little the Alaska Game Commission could do since only Congress could make a change. (The entire law was in the process of being chaged at the time of statehood but became moot when the state took control of its resources.)

Patrols involved driving along the road system and walking to the hunting areas checking licenses, legality of kills and acting at times as referees over fights of ownership of downed animals. I once held the rifles of two combatants who had it out because one had observed the other tearing floor boards from an old emergency cabin for use as firewood. I doubt if the one individual will ever tear up cabins again.

The quarter-mile-from-the-road regulation was an attempt to create a safety zone for nonhunters and motorists. Ray Woolford, my supervisor, had an interesting contact one day on the 40-Mile Road (known today as the Taylor Highway). There were numerous bands of caribou crossing the highway which tempted many to chance a kill from the roadway and remove the carcass before anyone came along. Ray was driving down the highway in a unmarked vehicle. As he drove around a curve he came upon a hunter leaning over the hood of his car taking aim at a caribou several hundred yards off. He shouted, "Hey you can't shoot from there."

The hunter quickly answered, "Yes, I can, I've got a scope." And with that squeezed off a round, killing the animal. Ray walked up and said, "That's not what I meant," and proceeded to write a violation notice for illegal taking. The chagrined hunter then had to pack the animal out and turn it in at the check station.

A few days later I was parked at a vantage point along the highway observing several bands of nice big bulls moving along a river bottom. There were several vehicles parked in the vicinity so I felt these animals would probably be taken before long. Sure enough, a barrage of rifle fire opened up about a half mile off in that direction. It sounded like a war had begun, and I lost track of the number of shots fired. I decided that I'd better check this group out as we had been finding many dead animals in the woods which were the result of herd shooting. Novice hunters would shoot into a group of animals rather than picking out one to kill. This resulted in crippling animals that were abandoned to die and rot in the woods.

When the shooting stopped I proceeded in that direction, whistling and making a great deal of noise so that I would not be mistaken for a caribou in the event the hunters had ammunition left. I finally located two hunters who were trying to gut out a nice bull and introduced myself. I asked how many animals had been taken and was surprised when they answered only three. They went on to explain that the third member of the party had gone to the car for packboards. When I questioned them about the number of shots, they meekly said this was the first hunt they had ever made and pointed out that they were poor shots. One said he fired six shots and the other said he shot at least 11 times at his animal. They went on to say that Bob, the other hunter, had used up a full box of ammo before getting his animal. I found this difficult to believe, so after checking the three dead caribou I scoured the surrounding area looking for additional kills or cripples. After 30 minutes of searching I found no evidence of any additional animals so I had to accept their story. I went back and found the two men still working on the first carcass.

After watching the proceedings for a few minutes I made a suggestion. It was obvious that the other two carcasses were beginning to bloat and needed immediate attention, so I recommended that they open them up and pull out the paunches. They agreed and as we walked over to the nearest animal they told me they were bartenders from Fairbanks. I sat down on a log to smoke my pipe and watched the proceedings. One of the men held onto a hind leg while the other grabbed his knife in both hands and said, "Well, here we go again." With that he plunged the knife into the abdomen cutting upwards causing the gas to burst out and spray both men with the stomach contents. I could not believe my eyes, nor could I sit and watch any longer, so I asked them to walk with me to the last animal. As they watched I took my knife and in a matter of minutes showed them how to open the cavity and remove the entrails without puncturing the paunch. When I finished, the fellow who had plunged the knife into the caribou paunch said to the other, "See, I told you there had to be a better way!"

I shook my head, said good-bye and walked back to the car. As I drove off I thought of the old adage, "You can take the boy out of the city but you can't take the city out of the boy."

One year we put the check station at Fox, just north of Fairbanks, to monitor the kills from both the Steese Highway and the Livengood Road. Not many caribou were being taken that year, but the moose hunting was fair and quite a few kills were coming through. The bird hunters were also doing well and had many limits of ptarmigan.

On a beautiful sunny September day during the middle of the week my good friend Max Bruton stopped after a day of bird hunting with his dog Lucky. Lucky was a hard-headed Labrador, a great retriever and just as stubborn as Max. Earlier in the season Max had trained Lucky to flush ptarmigan and retrieve them after they were shot. Retrieving was no problem for Lucky who was great in the duck marshes, but staying close to Max and flushing birds within shotgun range was more difficult. He just wasn't an upland hunter. On one occasion Max became so frustrated when Lucky roamed too far out that he gave him a blast of bird shot in the rear. Max agreed it was an unfortunate incident and costly in veterinarian bills to have the shot removed.

Lucky and Max stayed buddies, however, and here they were back from a successful hunt. Max was all smiles as he led me to the back of his station wagon to show me his day's take. His shotgun was on the floor pointing aft and the birds were piled in the corner. As we approached the rear of the vehicle Lucky, who had been sleeping, came to life and started bouncing up and down looking forward to getting out. As Max started rolling the back window of the station wagon down Lucky became more exuberant and one of his feet contacted the trigger of the presumed unloaded shotgun. There was a loud explosion and a load of bird shot blew a hole the size of a silver dollar through the tail gate, passing between Max and me, catching the pocket of Max's hunting jacket. In the pocket of his jacket he was carrying 3 shotgun shells which were discharged by the force of the shot, causing burns to his thigh. We were extremely fortunate not to have been seriously injured. Max was humiliated, and Lucky wasn't bothered at all; he just wanted out. A week later the story was out, and it has been written up several times in papers and magazines. The title always read, "Man Shoots Dog — Dog Shoots Man."

Both Max and Lucky are gone now, and it is to be hoped they are in the happy hunting grounds, still sharing adventures together.

Later that same week I was patrolling the Livengood Road on a beautiful Saturday morning. You see some strange things on hunting patrols, but even so, I was completely dumbfounded as I drove down toward the Chatanika River to see a Jeep coming up the hill carrying a whole bull moose. I mean the entire carcass, legs, head, antlers and all, with only the entrails removed. I turned my vehicle around and stopped the Jeep, which was badly overheating. Four soldiers got out. I looked, amazed, at the carcass which covered the entire cab, windshield, and hood, with the head and horns hanging over the radiator, and asked how they had managed to get it in place. Apparently, some buddies had helped them and being young and strong, they felt this was the best way to haul it. I asked who had shot it and one of them

took the credit and produced his hunting license. He told me how he had shot it and his partners confirmed the story. I wrote "1 moose" and the date with my initials on the back of his license. This would indicate that he had taken his limit on moose and was not entitled to another. We had no harvest tickets in those years. I then pointed out that the animal would sour rapidly if they didn't get the hide off and cut it into quarters soon. They told me they had a camp down the next mining road and would be taking care of the meat as soon as they arrived. I shook my head, turned around again and headed toward Livengood.

Later in the day I was enroute back to the check station and was waved down by two men standing by a flat bed truck. One was very excited and explained that he had shot a moose early in the morning and went to Fairbanks and hired a truck for transportation. When he returned, the moose was gone. I asked him how big the animal was, and after he described it I thought about the moose on the Jeep.

I invited him to go with me, and we drove down the old mine road where the GIs were supposed to be camped. We located them staying with an old-timer in a dilapidated cabin. The moose had been skinned and the quarters were hanging on a meat rack. I gathered everyone together and asked the four again about the taking of their moose. This time the story differed from the first account. After further discussion, they admitted that they had not killed it but found it shot and lying in the woods. I said obviously then this moose belongs to this man who shot it, cleaned it and then went for a truck to haul it back to Fairbanks. No, they said it couldn't be because this moose had been recently killed but had not been gutted.

Scratching my head, I turned to the hunter who was standing by the car and said, "You did gut it didn't you?"

"No," he said, "I didn't have a knife with me at the time."

I stared at him in disbelief and questioned him further, "How long did it take you to get to town, hire a truck and get back to the kill site?" He looked up sheepishly and stated he had been gone about six hours. "Jeez," I said, "that moose would have been soured by the time you returned, so as far as I'm concerned it belongs to these men who salvaged it." I marked his license with a moose taken, ending his hunt for the year, and told him he should thank the other hunters for saving him from getting a citation for wanton waste. I also lectured him about not going hunting again without the necessary equipment to take care of his kill. He went back to Fairbanks a much wiser man I'm sure.

There are many hunters who stop at the check station for advice on the best areas to hunt and request information on the regulations. One individual came into the 40-Mile check station wanting to know where he could go to shoot a wolf. How do you answer that one? Few wolves had been reported in the area by the predator control boys. Also, how often does anyone ever see a wolf in the wild? Very seldom, if ever. But being very professional, I pointed on a map to a large river that was mostly dried up that year. I suggested that many times wolves travel along dry river bars and by positioning himself on a high point of land he might be successful.

He left thanking me and I went back to work helping to weigh a bunch of caribou that had just arrived. The day was busy, and along toward evening I had taken a break to cook dinner when in popped the wolf hunter with a big gray wolf in his pickup. He had gone where I told him to, found a good location, and positioned himself where he could see in both directions for several miles. Sure enough, after several hours of patiently scanning with his binoculars a wolf came loping down the river bar and he nailed him with one shot. His comment to me was, "That was great, now tell me where I can get another one."

How do you figure it? To him, I was the greatest guide ever, and to me, he was the luckiest hunter of the season. ▪

Chapter 12

For the Want
of Snowshoes

W E DIDN'T NEED THEM last trip" we told each other, and
so began the unforgettable trip of the forgotten snowshoes.
It was to be a routine beaver-pelt sealing trip to the villages of
Ruby, Galena, Koyukuk, Nulato and Huslia, combined with a
patrol of some of the heavily trapped areas in-between. The date
was March 9, 1954, a beautiful clear day with the temperature
about -30°, and my partner was Jim King. We planned to use
the ski-equipped Piper Pacer because of its ability to get in and
out of small ice and snow-covered lakes or rivers where most
of the trapping activity was taking place. Our gear for the trip
was packed accordingly. First, there were 1,500 consecutively
numbered locking metal seals with the necessary affidavit books
carefully stacked in a canvas bag. Then came the travel
necessities, a rifle, emergency gear, sleeping bags, cameras, wing
covers, engine cover, a specially designed oil can for draining
the engine oil at night, a plumber's fire pot for pre-heating the
engine in the mornings, and our personal belongings to last for
five to seven days away from headquarters.

The ski-equipped Pacer was heated with the Herman Nelson
heaters at Fairbanks International Airport while we loaded the
gear. As we were preparing to depart, Jim noticed that we had
neglected to bring snowshoes. One never traveled without these
rawhide-laced wooden frames since they were the only means
of packing down a runway should the plane get bogged down.
To retrieve them would mean that one of us would have to drive
back to town costing us at least an hour's delay in our departure.
We were already behind schedule so the prospect of a further
delay was not encouraging. Then came the famous last words.

"We didn't need them last trip," which was true as very little snow had fallen this year. On our last patrol just the week before we had walked over much of that same area in only ankle deep snow which was highly unusual for this time of year. Because Interior Alaska was still under the influence of a large high pressure system with cold weather prevailing, we had no reason not to believe that conditions would be the same this trip. An unwise decision was made — we would go without the snowshoes.

I took off at 11:55 a.m. and headed west into flawless flying conditions. It was severe clear without a bump in the air and visibility was unlimited. We flew alongside Esther Dome, continued over the Minto flats and crossed the Tanana River at a cruising altitude of about 2,000 feet. The monotonous droning of the engine and the bright sun lulled Jim to sleep while I struggled to stay awake. We had both been out late the night before.

As we were crossing the Cossna River flats I remarked aloud that with visibility this clear, if anybody shot an illegal moose we would be able to see it five miles away. Jim cocked open his eyes, looked out the right window and remarked, "There's one right there." I banked the aircraft and sure enough there were two men butchering out a freshly killed moose. I circled the area as we planned a course of action. By backtracking their trail we found a tent camp about 3 miles from the kill and by following their main tracks to the north, determined that they were beaver trappers probably from the village of Tanana. There was only one area suitable for landing, a snow-covered meadow about halfway between the moose kill and the tent camp. Our plan was simple. After landing Jim would proceed to the kill site, and I would go to the tent camp to intercept the individuals involved, should they try to take off with their dog teams.

I evaluated the landing site and made a pattern over the spruce trees, easing the plane gently onto the snow patch. The aircraft settled and settled and settled, finally coming to rest in snow clear up to the windshield. It was impossible to taxi, for the Pacer was completely bogged down in loose, fluffy snow and when I shut down the engine the shock set in — *no snowshoes.* We had landed in a valley that had received substantially more snow than the rest of the country for some unknown reason. How would we get out? It was imperative that we make contact with the men we were pursuing as they had snowshoes and dog teams which made them mobile while we had no means of getting out of this valley of the deep snows. The time was 1:25 p.m.

The aircraft door was forced open and we made our way into the four-foot-deep powdery snow. Jim floundered off toward the moose kill while I made like a land otter, pushing my way to the tent. After three hours of half swimming or pulling myself through the willows I finally found the tent. All the time I was fighting my way to the camp I was worried about Jim who was going in the opposite direction. He would have to retrace his steps to get back to the plane, then follow my trail to the tent site. It was obvious that we would be spending the night here due to impending darkness.

As I was inspecting the tent camp an Indian trapper arrived and asked why I was there. I explained the situation about the moose kill and our plane. He said that the two trappers we had observed must be his partners and he confirmed that they were from Tanana. They had arrived at this location three days earlier after several days on the trail with two dog teams. Their venture would last several weeks, which was certainly speculative because unless they had another food cache somewhere the outfit he showed me was insufficient to sustain 3 men and 11 dogs for two weeks. When I questioned him about this he advised they planned to eat mostly beaver meat once the traps started producing. The high protein beaver carcasses would also feed the dogs, providing their traps produced. So far prospects didn't look very good, he admitted, which was the reason his partners left this morning on snowshoes to try and locate a moose.

After we had a good fire going in the tent I told him Jim and I were stuck for the night and would have to somehow make arrangements with him for our night's lodging. He looked around and I guess we both had the same question. How can five men sleep in a 8' x 10' wall tent equipped with a stove and cooking equipment? It was crowded quarters for just the three trappers, and two more bodies would be impossible. Somehow we would have to manage, though, so I went out and started cutting and splitting a rick of wood to last the night, for it would no doubt go down below -40° before morning.

Later the other two Indian trappers snowshoed into camp. I inquired about Jim, and they said he was enroute from the kill site and they were going back to pick him up with one of the dog teams. About an hour later in the darkness they were back with an exhausted Jim who agreed that the tent, as small as it was, looked mighty good.

After he rested we talked over our problems. Our concern was a place to spend the night and a runway for the aircraft. The Indians faced the charges of killing a cow moose out of season. We resolved the situation by offering to pay them to

snowshoe out a runway in the morning, and allowing us to stay the night in the tent. The illegal moose incident would be handled separately at a later date in Tanana and would not be an issue at this time. Both of our sleeping bags were in the airplane and we decided not to ask our hosts to make another trip with their team to recover them since there was not enough room to stretch out five people. It would be a matter of keeping the fire going all night with Jim and me sitting up, making ourselves as comfortable as possible.

We busied ourselves with wood cutting while the trappers

cooked their evening meal. This additional exercise sharpened our already keen appetites, but unfortunately there was little prospect for a meal this night. The meager supplies and strained relationship with our new associates did not give much prospect for filling our empty stomachs. All we had of our own were emergency rations back in the plane, and like the sleeping bags, we did not think it was wise to ask them to hook up the dogs. We stacked all the split spruce near the front of the tent where it would be easy to reach during the long night ahead.

By nine o'clock we were finished and poked our heads through the tent flap to observe the three trappers finishing a slim meal of rice and biscuits. We entered the crowded quarters after taking off our heavy outer clothing and tried to make ourselves as inconspicuous as possible. After they finished they gave us each a biscuit, some tea and what was left of the rice. This did little for the hunger pangs but would take care of our needs until we got back to town.

The night proved to be exceptionally long and cold. While the three trappers slept nice and snug in their sleeping bags, we dozed sitting up, in fits and starts, with the stove going from hot to cold as the wood burned out. The tent would cool immediately causing one of us to wake with a start to fill it with wood again. When daylight finally came we both looked like we had been dragged through a knothole.

Their breakfast consisted of some dried fish which served as dog food also, while we had to settle for growling stomachs. Finally the dogs were hooked up and the five of us proceeded to the plane with the two dog teams. Jim and I rode while the drivers walked behind the sleds helping it through the tangled alder brush. One of them walked ahead on snowshoes breaking trail. At the plane they immediately went to work snowshoeing out a runway about 500 feet long while we pre-heated the aircraft engine and oil with the firepot. The skis were dug out, propped and scraped clean of the frost that had built up during the night. It was important to have these surfaces polished for fast acceleration since the runway was not going to be any too long. What we wanted was enough packed-down snow for the plane to build up the speed necessary for the wings to start developing lift. This would then allow the skis to run on top of the powdered snow until take-off speed was attained.

The runway was finished and the plane engine started and

The runway was finished and the plane engine started and warmed sufficiently for normal operation. Then with Jim and the trappers pushing I was able to get the aircraft positioned for a take-off run. We said our good-byes and told the trappers we would fly back over the camp in two days with whatever supplies they requested as exchange for the lodging and work performed. The supplies would be air dropped, so anything breakable was out. They went into a huddle for about 5 minutes and gave us the group decision: 2 cartons of cigarettes. Jim and I looked at each other in disbelief and asked if they were kidding. They said no, that they would be getting plenty of beaver which would provide food and with the season ending March 30th, they would be home in Tanana in just over 3 weeks. We agreed and advised them that we would be dropping the cigarettes plus some grub, as requested. We also told them we would meet them in Tanana about April 15th to take care of the illegal moose situation and that the U.S. Commissioner would be told of the cooperation they had given us.

It took three tries to get airborne. Jim and the trappers had to assist after each attempt by pushing the taxiing plane back through the deep powdered snow to the new runway. Finally, we were off and with great relief we headed back to Fairbanks. The first thing we did was get a big meal. It was then that Jim told me that the moose they had killed was a sick one with big cysts in the lungs; it wasn't fit to eat.

What a series of events: A sick moose met its demise because three trappers went on a beaver hunting expedition without adequate supplies, and a routine landing could have turned into a nightmare because two experienced wardens forgot to take snowshoes.

We met the trappers in Tanana as pre-arranged and kept our part of the bargain. The U.S. Commissioner listened to our story when we filed the complaints and allowed the trappers to pay a minimum fine with the understanding that in the future they would plan trapping expeditions with more adequate supplies.

As for us, we never forgot snowshoes again. In fact, maybe I went overboard, for one of our aircraft mechanics was later overheard asking another, "How come Ray keeps snowshoes in his plane until it's time to go on floats?"

Chapter 13

Wolf Control

O NE OF THE MOST CONTROVERSIAL programs of the Fish & Wildlife Service in the 1950s was the killing of wolves by the Division of Predator & Rodent Control. Wolves were taken by aerial shooting and by the use of poisons, both strychnine and cyanide. Most of the hunting fraternity agreed with the need for control and supported the taking of wolves by shooting. Others were apathetic, feeling that the Fish and Wildlife Service knew what it was doing and shrugged it off as their business, not ours. Preservationists were a relatively small, elite group and any opposition from that quarter had little effect. Poison, however, was a different story and was either reluctantly supported or violently opposed. There seemed to be no middle ground.

The very word "poison" is enough to throw a fear into the majority of people, and rightly so. The fear of the unknown is born into all of us, and I must confess that even though I was indoctrinated into the use of poison baits and cyanide guns, I was never comfortable working with these lethal chemicals. The strychnine crystals used were about the size of a peanut and were shipped in small cardboard cylinders. They were prepared by forming a spoonful of lard into a ball about one inch in diameter and pushing a crystal into the center. The ball was then rolled into a brown, dry scented mixture of seal meal, giving it an attractive smell to the carnivores. They were then packaged in small paper bags with about 20 to a sack. These were set out at bait stations usually at a location where wolves had killed a moose or caribou.

Cyanide, on the other hand, is a powder which when used to take wolves and coyotes is placed in a .38 (or .357) caliber shell covered with wax to keep it intact. The shell is placed in a triggered cylinder set in the ground. A baited top is the only part exposed. When a wolf or coyote grabs the bait and pulls on it the shell is fired, forcing the poison into its throat. These were summer baits, and the lard balls were the winter baits.

The Fish and Wildlife Service in Alaska was understaffed in every division, so we all wore several hats. Thus, as an enforcement agent I helped tag fish with the sports fish biologist, made game counts, assisted in trapping animals alive, collected jaw bones with the game biologist, and counted migrating salmon with the commercial fish biologists. Another job was assisting the predator agents to control wolf populations. When I first took over the McGrath district, I had the help of Harley King, who was with the predator division. For six months he assisted me with the enforcement program, and I helped him with the wolf program. When he terminated his job no replacement was hired due to the lack of funds, so I was alone doing both jobs until two years later when another enforcement agent, Chuck Heimier, was hired. Together we carried on with the wolf program in those areas designated by the regional director.

One thing should be understood. I am not putting a stamp of approval on the wolf control program conducted by the Fish and Wildlife Service in the fifties. Rather, I am submitting the facts as I remember them and the reader can draw his own conclusions as to the merits of the program. The word control is important because it directed the policy and guidelines under which we operated. I have heard many accusations over the years that the Fish and Wildlife Service killed wolves by scattering poison indiscriminately out of airplanes over most of Alaska. That's pure hogwash. For one thing, there were on-going studies conducted by trained biologists which dictated the areas that needed a balance between the game animals and wolf populations. Wherever a large buildup of wolves was known to be preying on low stocks of moose or caribou a plan was put into effect to reduce wolf numbers in favor of the game animals. Prime target areas were those supporting herds hunted by subsistence users and the more popular hunting areas of urban hunters. Also important is the fact that the control programs were not annihilation schemes, but an attempt to remove the surplus predators and allow a buildup of ungulates.

Shooting was the number one method of taking wolves. Most

hunting was conducted from Supercub aircraft using Winchester Model 12 shotguns firing magnum loads of number 4 buckshot. These were special shells loaded for the Fish and Wildlife Service and contained 41 pellets instead of the usual 28. The gunner sat in the rear seat of the tandem aircraft and opened the side window for shooting, hoping he could kill the running wolf without hitting either the prop or the wing strut. This occurred more than once with even experienced gunners in the heat of a chase, with varying effects on the aircraft. Some had to land and wait repairs while others limped back to home base with an unbalanced propeller. It took good teamwork to be effective as the gunner had to completely trust the pilot's ability to keep

the plane from stalling or hitting trees while he concentrated on shooting. This required a negative lead because the plane flew faster than the wolf and was quite tricky since animals seldom run in a straight line. We had gunners who were capable of taking several wolves in one pass under the right conditions, which is no easy feat while hanging by a seat belt. The pilot on the other hand, had to trust the gunner completely so he didn't have to worry about stray shots hitting his prop, or more seriously, the wing strut, which could cause the wing to fail as he flew low and slow dodging obstructions while making passes over the running wolves. At times, especially when the snow was deep causing the animals to run in a single trail, a good gunner would take as many as five wolves before they dispersed. Other times on hard packed snow and especially in timbered country, several passes might be necessary to kill one wolf as it dodged and ran into the cover of the trees.

The most successful hunters were the pilots who could track. Seldom were wolves found by randomly flying around the countryside but rather by being able to identify wolf tracks or trails and systematically following them to the critters themselves. This was seldom an easy chore since wolves are capable of traveling up to 50 miles in a 24 hour period in search of food. Once a track was cut the direction of travel was determined, not always an easy job especially in deep snow, and the pursuit began. If the tracks went through dense timber a great deal of time could be lost in finding where they came out. Other times they might become obliterated in a maze of moose or caribou trails, and the pilot had to circle and sift out the signs in the snow to determine the route taken or the location of kill if one was made. Kills were often found by observing ravens which took over possession of the dead animals once the wolves finished gorging. On and on, the tracking continued with a great deal of banking, turning and other maneuvering, requiring an iron stomach on the part of the gunner.

Once wolves were sighted, the real excitement began. Picture yourself sitting behind your pilot when he yells "There they are." At that moment you open the hinged door on your right which on a Supercub is in two sections, one which folds up attaching to a wing fitting and the other hanging down leaving a section about 2½ feet high by 4 feet wide exposed to the outside air. Should the temperature be in the below zero range (we hunted in the -40s at times to take advantage of the clear weather), it is exhilirating to say the least, and vital that hands be adequately protected when handling the shotgun. This is especially important in reloading, which cannot be done with mittens. Even gloves are a nuisance in trying to handle slippery shells. Never mind your face since you have a fur lined hat with the ear flaps tied under the chin to keep it in place and it is not quite in the main air blast anyway. Frozen noses and eyelids are part of the job, and you get little sympathy from the pilot who is lining up for a pass at tree top level and who is shouting for you to get ready.

The quarry may be anywhere from one to a dozen or more wolves. We once tackled a pack of 18, but this was an exception. If the snow is deep and they are in single file you start with the rear wolf and work forward, downing as many as possible before they scatter. In hard packed snow or ice they will usually scatter at the sound of your approaching engine, so you seek an individual and have to be satisfied with one or two shots per pass. At the end of the run your pilot will do a turning maneuver and as your cheeks bulge and stomach churns you feed shells into the magazine, making sure the muzzle of the shotgun is pointing away from critical parts of the plane. Then it's another pass at the scattered animals causing the pilot to zig and zag the aircraft to get into shooting position and keep the animal from reaching the timber. As you shoot you must keep remembering negative lead and at the same time try to anticipate a wolf's leap left or right. You miss and the pilot curses, but he knows it is all part of the game. His maneuvers become even more abrupt now, and the only time the needle and ball of the turn coordinator instrument are together is when they're passing each other. That's not your problem, however. You trust the pilot, and you keep reminding yourself that over and over as you shake your head clear of the blood that's been forced against the cranium. To relieve the tension you might yell "Where did you get your license, Sears and Roebuck?" Round and round you go until all the wolves are dispatched or the remaining animals are so scattered in the timber that additional hunting is a waste of effort. If you are in mountain areas or rolling hills with few trees it may be possible to keep tracking each animal until all are taken, but a low fuel supply usually dictates a hasty retreat back to camp before this can be accomplished.

As the pilot you're flying and tracking skills determine the success of the mission. Your eyes are taxed to the limit as you try to decipher track patterns in the snow as you depend on peripheral vision to keep the plane from exceeding the structual limits imposed by the manufacturer. Once the wolves are spotted you take on the role of a fighter pilot, twisting, turning and dodging trees, hills and canyon walls as you get the plane lined up for the gunner. If he misses a few times your patience wears thin and you try to maneuver closer to help him out. You might even shout out endearing phrases such as "Have you had your eyes checked lately?" or "Is the barrel bent on that shotgun?"

Once the shooting is over you have another task — making a successful landing so the kills can be retrieved. This is not always easily accomplished, especially in mountainous or hilly terrain. Often it's necessary to snowshoe several miles back to hills, or in especially difficult terrain, kills have to be abandoned. Every effort is made to get to the animals as this is an important part of the job. The wolves have to be skinned (later sold at auction), not an easy chore in cold weather, and biological data collected. Measurements and weights are taken and the skull and stomach contents sacked and labeled for further study. Then it is back to camp where the plane has to be fueled and tied down with wood blocks or poles under the skis to keep them from freezing down. The oil has to be drained and the wing and engine covers put on so all will be ready for another flight tomorrow. This goes on day after day until the wolves have either been thinned out of the target area or the weather closes in, prohibiting flying.

Several of the sacks containing prepared strychnine baits were taken along on each flight, and if a wolf kill was located, it was baited. A landing was made in the vicinity if possible, and the kill site studied to determine the number of wolves in the pack, age and condition of the moose or caribou. Baits were then carefully distributed around the remains. I say *carefully* because the errant notion is that we just threw baits all around that would eventually kill everything in sight. First, we worked under the known fact that the wolves would be back, because they always return to kill sites time and again as they make the rounds of their territory. Even after there is nothing left but bones they will make a visit to check "their property." We knew, too, that they are extremely inquisitive and like any canine have an extremely well-developed sense of smell. They would find the baits no matter where we hid them. So we would hide them away from the actual remains and under pieces of skin or hair so they wouldn't be obvious to birds and small mammals.

There is no denying that other game besides wolves were killed. Foxes were the most frequent. However, as foxes live their entire lives within a territory of only five miles, it stands to reason that only the few living in the immediate vicinity would become victims. Birds were a different story and ravens and magpies were frequent losers; however, when adding the pluses and the minuses, the loss of these other predators had to be considered as the cost of doing business. Occasionally a bear would succumb, but most of them were in hibernation during the time of year that strychnine was used. In the event there was a heavy predation by wolves in areas not conducive to hunting, or where the terrain made landings impossible, we were directed to sacrifice a caribou or moose and bait the carcass. After the target area was studied an animal was shot on a lake closest to the hunting territory of the wolves and baited. The reason for choosing a lake site was to make sure the baits would be destroyed faster in the spring when the ice went out. Normally the heat of summer melted the lard and rendered the baits useless, however, the process was stepped up whenever possible.

There were times when a fresh kill was located from the air in a key area where it was impossible to land within walking distance, which made it a candidate for an air drop. Prior to baiting, however, it was necessary to fly the entire vicinity to assure there was no human activity present. Trappers did not take kindly to having a poisoned bait located anywhere near their trapping activities. Once it was determined the area qualified, several low passes were made and the sacks dropped near the kill. Again the baits were placed away from the site, knowing that the wolves would find them even when they became snow-covered, whereas the birds and other smaller animals were more prone to feed on the kill itself.

This was not a desired method of taking wolves and only resorted to whenever there was no other way of knocking down a population in a critical area. It opened the door to a great deal of criticism by the public. The consequences had to be weighed carefully and the regional office kept apprised of each air drop since they were responsible for answering complaints from irate citizens.

Some complaints were justified, especially when a kill was baited in a controversial area or too close to human habitation. On several occasions a clean up crew was sent into a misplaced site to pick up all the baits.

There were also the unjustified complaints from people who were completely opposed to any killing or the use of poison. When I say unjustified I do not refer to the right to disagree or oppose the policy of wolf control or the use of lethal agents, but to the spreading of falsehoods to the news media. This accomplished nothing except to create a mud slinging contest;

however, any documented cases of improprieties by Fish and Wildlife Service employees brought results and changes in operating procedures. Also, as public attitude changed so did the entire program and during the last few years prior to statehood there was more research going on than actual killing. An example is the study of the Nelchina wolves. After taking most of the wolves from that area to allow a buildup of the caribou herd, aerial surveys indicated that there was only one pack of nine animals left. For the next two years all control work was halted and agent Bob Burkholder spent most of his time following the pack and documenting their travels and kills.

Another accusation hurled at the Fish and Wildlife Service was that it used 1080 poison for the taking of wolves. There was no truth in this, and in fact there was a strict policy against its use for anything but for exterminating disease-carrying rats in municipal dump sites. Ten-eighty was used on coyotes in some western states by killing a horse or cow and injecting the poison into the bloodstream. Any animal eating the carcass became a victim. I don't know of any case where it was used on wolves.

I had to investigate a bitter complaint from a Fairbanks citizen in the early 1960s concerning the use of 1080 by one of the predator control agents. He had responded to a serious problem of a rat-infested dump at the University of Alaska. The rats were invading the campus, causing a great deal of concern to the administrators. The agent agreed to poison the dump with 1080 with the understanding that the dump would be covered by bulldozer within 24 hours from the time the bait boxes were put out. The boxes were built of wood and had openings only large enough for the rats. After eating they usually died a short distance away but within the confines of the dump. Unfortunately, there was a communication problem and the person responsible for covering the site apparently did not get the message. Several days went by and dogs started eating some of the dead rats, causing death or violent sickness. According to the complainants their dog came home and vomited in the yard. The vomit was picked by some exotic birds which soon died. It was not a nice scene and caused a great deal of flack before the situation died down.

Cyanide guns were set out on ridges, mountain passes and other routes wolves traveled. They were usually pulled up in the fall, however. I am aware that some were not retrieved or could not be found. Signs were posted warning people to keep dogs out of the area in the event a hunting party wandered through. Even so, I remember when a hunter up on the Charley River pulled one out of curiosity and it exploded in his hand. His friends ran the boat back to Circle and drove with great haste back to Fairbanks, a distance of 150 miles, thinking he would die. He didn't, but his hand was hurt and the accident ruined their hunting trip. The interesting thing was that they had read the warning sign before he had grabbed the shell to find out how it worked.

The program ended with statehood except for some continued control work around the reindeer herds on the Seward Peninsula. This was done under an agreement with the Bureau of Indian Affairs and the Department of Fish and Game. Also at the time of statehood the big game populations were in the best shape they had been in 20 years. Was it because of the wolf control program? There are those who believe without question that this was so; others, including many Fish and Game biologists, do not.

Predator control was stopped because of the feeling that wolves were important in cutting out the sick and the weak, a needed component in nature's balance. Years later after a large buildup in wolves were competing with hunters for diminishing moose and caribou herds, state Fish and Game biologists initiated another control program. This was met with great resistance by some members of the public, including school children. Law suits were filed to stop some wolf hunts by the state. Due to the environmentalists and the prevailing Disney image of wolves, it is difficult to get total public support for thinning wolf packs in areas of heavy predation. As for poison bait stations, I'm sure that this will never be allowed in Alaska again.

The program as it was approved by the Alaska Game Commission and administered by the U.S. Fish and Wildlife Service was not without merit and was highly successful. It was not an all-out destruction program, but one based on sound scientific evidence collected by employees who had a great deal of respect and admiration for the wolf. Somehow wolf numbers will have to be controlled again if a healthy population of moose and caribou is to be maintained. He is too keen a competitor to be ignored. The methods and means are available to the game manager today. His biggest challenge and obstacle is to somehow educate the public and gain its support. This can only be accomplished by a well-planned information and education program that will have to be undertaken regardless of the cost if control is to succeed.█

Chapter 14

Animal Control

IN ADDITION TO HUNTING WOLVES as an agent I was also required to do other types of control work that made the rifle and shotgun just as important in this job as they were when I was a professional trapper. Included in the taking were rogue bears, crippled and diseased animals and specimens collected for museums and wildlife laboratories. Some of the kills were a challenge, requiring precision shooting, while with others, such as with crippled animals, it was only a matter of walking up and dispatching the critters at close range to put them out of their misery. Lest the reader get the idea that this was all fun and games, let me assure you it was not. In fact, at times there was a considerable amount of hard work connected with it, and it was not always very rewarding.

Moose that were crippled as a result of collisions with cars, trucks or trains were always given a priority to minimize suffering. Unfortunately for us, it seemed that at least 90 percent of these occurred at night and usually when it was extremely cold. Most of the time the moose had broken legs and were not far from the site of the accident; however, occasionally they wandered off and had to be tracked down. This was not always easy, especially if there was little or no snow and only a light blood trail. Throw in a temperature of -40° or lower and it becomes about as unpleasant a job as anyone wants to have. If we located the moose we had to determine the extent of injuries and decide whether or not to shoot the animal. If it was to be killed we positioned ourselves for a quick brain shot to end the suffering immediately.

I learned early in my career that the issue .38 caliber revolver was next to worthless for such work. The massive bone structure protecting a small brain can cause the bullet to change its course even at close range making the shot ineffective. This occurred with my first road-crippled moose that was down with two broken legs. At least 20 people had collected at the scene when I arrived, all waiting to see me do my duty. I walked up with great poise, drew my service .38 and placed five shots where I felt the brain should be, all to no avail. Imagine my chagrin as I had to walk back to my vehicle for a shotgun which then finished the job. A hero I was not, but I had learned a valuable lesson and never used a .38 again on a crippled animal. Years later we were issued .357 magnums which were much more effective. I also found that a better technique was to have a partner keep the animal's attention while approaching from the rear, placing the bullet in the area where the cervical vertebra joins the back of the skull.

I had a similar problem with a .38 caliber revolver years later, trying to dispatch a black bear that was caught in a snare. This occurred at Ohtig Lake, about 35 miles northeast of Fort Yukon. I was in charge of a crew that was banding flightless ducks to determine the effects on wildlife of a proposed dam on the Yukon River. Over a period of six days we built a trap 100 feet long by 25 feet wide and captured more than 10,000 diving ducks, mostly scaup, golden eye, buffleheads and canvasbacks. It took three days to remove, weigh, measure and band each bird. Meanwhile we were plagued by two black bears messing up our equipment and munching up the few weak ducks. The bears became so brazen they walked into the camp while we worked, prompting us to declare war before someone was hurt. We set a snare made from parachute cord on the incoming trail, not really thinking out what we would do if a bear got caught. However, within 15 minutes we were faced with a serious problem. The larger of the bears came into camp, placing his head directly in the noose and was immediately captured. He became enraged and started tearing up all the terrain within his reach. It was then that we checked our equipment only to learn that no one had a weapon. We were not in the habit of carrying firearms on these operations since we had not previously been bothered by any critters.

One of our crew was a local trapper hired for this project. He indicated he had a .38 revolver in one of his line camps on the Porcupine River not too far from our location. I loaded him up in one of the float planes and flew him to the cabin. We returned with the well-used and rusted weapon to find the crew watching the bear from what they considered a safe distance. By now he was not fighting the noose but was still not in what you would call a good mood. Since I was the crew leader and most experienced with firearms I was elected, by a very undemocratic vote, to take care of our newly acquired team member. As I approached he became very alert and after several circles it was evident that I would only be allowed a front on head shot. A carefully aimed shot placed between his eyes which did not even knock him down. It just infuriated him. Watching him go into action, tearing up the remaining willows and stunted spruce trees in his reach, chilled me. I have no idea why the nylon cord didn't break. (I can attest to the fact that parachute cord is strong.) Fortunately he wasn't a large bear, probably weighing only 250 pounds, or the outcome would likely have been different. I was finally able to work my way to his blind side and place another shot behind the ear, which did the job. With a great sigh of relief we went back to work and completed the banding late that night.

We butchered the bear and took the meat to a Native village where it was gladly accepted and divided among some of the more needy families. Later we boiled up the skull and checked it carefully to determine the damage of the two shots. The second had entered the brain causing instant death. The first, even though it entered the front of the skull in line with the brain, had been deflected by the thick bone and angled out the side with little effect except to give him a giant headache. That was the last time I used a .38 for anything except target practice. There may be a message here for those who pack side arms for protection against bears.

That was a particularly bad year for black bears. Apparently there was a high population of bears coupled with a shortage of forage. One miner was killed and eaten in the Manley Hot Springs area and one of our biologists checking study plots adjacent to where we were banding got chased up a tree and had his foot badly chewed up. There were several other attacks that summer, including two campers mauled in a tent. Blackies are dangerous, although many people disregard this fact, including the miner who had lived in Alaska all his life. From all appearances, he had tried to chase the bear off with a broom and ended up paying the ultimate price. They may not have the nasty temper of a grizzly, but pound for pound a black bear can be just as mean under the right conditions.

In my survival kit I carried a .22 revolver with the idea that it could be used for birds or rabbits in an emergency. I had the opportunity to use it several times on crippled moose out in the bush and found it to be much more effective than the .38. In March 1955, Jim King and I landed near a moose that had fallen through some shelf ice on a slough at the mouth of the Dalby River. Jim had spotted the animal several times over a period of a week flying between the villages of Koyukuk and Huslia. The moose had not moved and appeared to be lying in the same spot, which is highly unusual. Enroute to Huslia the following week we detoured and checked the area again and found him still there. This time we landed and found a very emaciated animal with no control over his hind legs, which appeared to be broken. There was no water left in the slough which had gone dry after freeze-up, leaving the ice hanging with little strength. The animal had been trapped without food for at least 10 days that we were aware of. We concluded he had suffered greatly because of the thrash marks in the snow. He must have been one tough moose to have lived so long. I went back to the plane and dug out the .22 revolver from my gear. One shot put the large animal out of its misery, which surprised me because I had some concern about using the small caliber revolver. On several other occasions I used this same weapon with excellent results. However, these were all crippled animals unable to move. I certainly would never recommend it as anything but a survival gun, and then only for small game. It is definitely not a gun to be used for defense against bears, and in my estimation neither is the .357 or .44 magnum. Having been in the business for years and observing many defense-of-life situations, the only weapon that is effective at close range, in my estimation, is a shotgun loaded with buckshot.

I used a .357 magnum one time on a moose crippled by wolves. The call came in from a concerned citizen in Copper Center to Red James, the Department of Fish and Game officer in Glennallen. I had been flying several tons of grain into the area to eliminate a starvation problem for the migrating ducks in the Copper River valley. Mother Nature had played a cruel trick, dropping temperatures down to the zero mark on the first of May in 1964 bringing a cold snap that lasted several days. This in turn froze all the ponds and sloughs used by the birds for feeding and caused their death by the thousands. Alaska sportsmen rallied and purchased cracked corn and other grain to distribute to the areas hardest hit. I remained in Glennallen several days helping Red distribute the feed and caring for the many emaciated ducks we were to pick up.

When the call came in concerning the crippled moose we drove to the location and searched the surrounding woods until we spotted the animal. It was obviously in bad shape and gaping wounds on one shoulder were evident as she hobbled along. The torn hide was evidence of an attack by a wolf or wolves. Although they missed a meal they were successful in causing her a great deal of suffering. I walked within 10 feet of the animal and squeezed the trigger of my brand new, very expensive, never used before .357 magnum revolver. All I got was a click and then two clicks more before it finally fired, killing the moose immediately. Good thing this isn't a life threatening situation, I told Red, and he enthusiastically nodded in agreement.

Back in Glennallen we test fired the revolver and found that it misfired about every eighth shot. I shipped it back to the factory where the gunsmith determined that the main spring was not snapping the hammer down hard enough to detonate the shell. So much for expensive weapons, but at least it did finally do its job and saved the moose many days of unnecessary suffering.

Like oil and water, bears and man just do not mix. One of the best ways to prove this is to put in an open pit dump next to a military site in the Bush and leave it unattended. A large quota of bears that will come from miles around to feed on the great amounts of exposed garbage. If the food supply runs low the ever hungry bruins will follow their noses to the kitchen area of the camp, and sooner or later they will break into buildings searching for something to eat. Added to this are the inquisitive personnel who are anxious for pictures to send home. They usually entice the animals in closer with food, sometimes hand held. The inevitable occurs, and someone either gets mauled, or the camp commander has to account for all the funds he keeps spending on new doors and windows. The next step is to call the nearest wildlife agent and ask him to get rid of the bears.

STD

At McGrath I answered many such complaints from the several remote radar sites scattered throughout the district. Mostly they concerned black bears, but occasionally the offender was a grizzly. Sometimes the problem could be solved through radio communication by advising the commander to use scare tactics involving flares and other pyrotechnics. This worked occasionally, but if the bear or bears were well established, it was only a temporary solution. Eventually I would have to make a trip to the establishment and spend a few days sizing up the problem, making suggestions for long term solutions and ridding the area of the problem bears.

The first requirement was a tour of the base checking the buildings, established trails, and the dump. Any time there was a dump that was not being burned daily and covered continually with dirt the bears congregated. This was discussed with the commander who would usually take the appropriate measure. However, some showed little interest, and if on subsequent visits there was no improvement, the matter was taken to headquarters. This always brought results, and I never failed to get backing from the commanding officers from then on. I always spent one evening showing a few wildlife movies to the personnel, followed by a lecture on the dangers of feeding wild animals which was illustrated by slides of mauled victims. Additionally, I warned of the ever present problem of feeding and making pets of the cute foxes found at camp kitchens with a talk on rabies and the painful treatment to those who had been bitten. I always ended with a discussion of my job and responsibilities, making the point that although I was a wildlife protector, I was now being forced into the role of wildlife destroyer because of carelessness.

The final task was that of killing the bears. This might take one day or several depending on the number involved. If there was no dump involved I located the trail where the intruder entered the compound and picked out a spot to shoot from that would assure no danger to any of the electronic equipment of facilities. After that I questioned those who knew the most about the bears' habits and positioned myself on location during the most opportune hours. When bruin showed up a well placed shot ended his military career. It was unfortunate because he was simply a victim of circumstances, being in the wrong place at the wrong time, but there was no other way, and death was his reward for trying to survive in man's environment.

There were times when the bears were so numerous it seemed the entire population for hundreds of miles was congregated in the one area. Such was the case one summer at Tatalina Air Force Base, a radar site located about 10 miles from McGrath. The military ran a sloppy dump that year, and a large number of black bears were feeding on the raw garbage being disposed of daily. When I received the call for help I surveyed the problem with several high ranking officers from the Alaska Command of Anchorage. I explained that trying to capture the bears and move them would be costly and time-consuming. The Fish and Wildlife Service could not afford it. After outlining what was entailed, including manpower, cost of traps and crates, plus the airpower needed to move the animals to another location, it was determined that it was not within the military's budget either. There was only one solution, and it was not in the best interest of the bears. I was assured complete cooperation and promised that some of the bears would be butchered and transported to a few Native villages by the military. The dump was located about a mile from the base, so I did not have to worry about shots endangering buildings or electronic equipment. Bear trails entered from several different directions like the spokes of a wheel so I made myself a blind out of packing crates at the entrance, giving me control over the entire area. There I waited throughout the day and night dispatching every bear that made his appearance. By the next day 14 blackies had been removed, which must have been the biggest part of the dump population since several subsequent trips netted only 2 more. The biggest were butchered; several weighed at least 500 pounds. It was interesting that when we examined the stomach contents of the bears there was every type of garbage imaginable. Included were waxed paper lables, tar paper, nails, pieces of metal, leather, wood and of course a variety of undigested foods. Some were so fat their stomachs appeared to drag on the ground. A few showed the scars of cuts received from the breaking and entering operations that caused all this one-sided war. There could only be one winner, and unfortunately for the lords of the forest, they would continue to lose even though it was their domain that had been invaded.

After I finished my part of the operation the military went to work by burning and covering the dump daily. Regulations directed to all personnel prohibited the feeding of any wild animals. Other bases had problems and one or two bears were removed, but none had the problem of such a large number of bears as Tatalina.

The military and its machinery caused other problems for wildlife which in turn added to our work load. For the most part they were very cooperative, especially when one of the troops violated the game laws. Not only did the individual face civil proceedings, but in many cases he was also required to drop rank and lose privileges. Such was the case of a captain helicoter pilot who shot a sheep northwest of Kotzebue. A picture of the officer, a dead sheep, and his helicopter was anonymously sent to our office in Fairbanks. I took the photo to the commanding officer at Ladd Field and explained our concern of taking a sheep out of season with the use of a helicopter. He had the picture blown up, identified the officer, and had him removed from duty until I arrived Kotzebue. There the captain pleaded guilty before the U.S. Commissioner and received a substantial fine. He told me later that in addition to the civil fine, he lost his captain's rank and was removed from his unit and given a desk job. Other cases ended in much the same way.

Bombing ranges took their share of game even though precautions were taken. One such instance involved a high altitude bombing run by several aircraft at Big Delta. The target was a bunch of oil drums located on the Delta River. The planes started at high altitude and dove on the target releasing 500-pound bombs from a predesignated height above the ground. Unfortunately during the early morning hours a group of buffalo moved out on the ice in the general vicinity of the drums. One of the planes zeroed in on the buffalo thinking they were the target as he made his speed dive and released the bombs, making a direct hit. As I recall, six or seven animals died instantly and an unknown number were wounded. Several of us were sent to the area to check for crippled buffalo and if possible determine the number involved. The seriously injured were to be dispatched immediately and survivors were to be observed to determine the extent of injuries. We spent about a week in the area tracking and locating six which were dragging broken legs. These were mercifully shot with only one fit for salvage and human consumption. We saw a few others that showed signs of having sustained injuries but capable of surviving. These were photographed and we reported back to headquarters. Several days later I was in the area on an investigation and found another cripple which had to be shot. This one had a gaping hole in its side with part of the intestines trailing. The animal was in terrible shape, with nothing in its stomach and it was difficult to believe it had lived 10 days in that condition. Another case of wildlife and man not living very well in harmony, with the animals being the losers as usual.

During the fall of 1954 I was given the assignment of killing one of the old male bison from the Big Delta herd for a full mount which was to be displayed at the museum of the University of Alaska. Since I had no experience in skinning and preparing an animal that size for a museum I requested and was granted the assistance of Frank Glaser. Frank was with the predator division and the old timer of the outfit, having been in Alaska since the early 1900s. He was an ex-professional hunter having made a living in the 1920s by providing the road commission crews at Black Rapids with fresh wild meat. He was paid 50¢ per pound for sheep and 25¢ per pound for moose and caribou, which he had to kill and pack out to designated drop-off spots. A team of horses and wagon would transport the meat the rest of the way to the camps. He spent his winters trapping in the Savage River country. He also did big game guiding and was hired for special projects by the Fish and Wildlife Service. One of these was a winter's stay on Nunivak Island making a count of the musk-ox by foot and dog team. Other assignments took him all over Alaska and he kept us entertained with his yarns of the "good old days." It was my pleasure to spend many days in the field with this venerable hunter. He was the last of his breed, and I cherished every day I spent with him.

On this particular trip we spent several days driving around trying to locate an old solitary bull beyond breeding age that would fill the requirements of the permit issued to the university. My wife of only a few months was able to join the expedition as the official photographer and scribe. Once the bull was killed there were copious measurements that had to be taken both before and after skinning, and Elsie recorded these on two different forms.

After three or four days of combing the area a fine specimen was located and taken. The skinning and measuring job required many hours with Elsie recording all the information with both pencil and camera. It was an excellent training session for me by the master, which I was to put to use many times in future years. The standing mount is on display and viewed by many visitors each year.

In 1958 I was sent to Nunivak Island to collect a large solitary bull musk-ox for the same museum. This time the animal was located from the air in late March from a ski-equipped Cessna 180. The weather was cold and clear which was unusual considering high winds and poor visibility are not uncommon in that part of Alaska. I landed as close as I dared to the animal without scaring him off and walked to his location about half a mile away. He was easily taken, and I then returned to the village of Mekoryuk to pick up several Natives to help with the skinning. Measurements and pictures were taken in accordance with instructions from Jonas Bros. of Denver, the taxidermy firm which mounted all specimens for the university. They gave explicit instructions requiring exact measurements since they had never handled a full mount musk-ox before and were anxious to do a good job. This was not an easy task in the sub-zero weather with a steaming carcass to work with. The Eskimos were a happy crew, however, and had butchered many animals including hundreds of reindeer from the island's herd, so they took it all in stride. They also knew they would have an opportunity to eat many fine steaks from the animal. The head was the most difficult part of the operation because of the way the horns angle downward, close to the skull. Knowing this would take many hours in itself, the hide was removed with the head attached and the job finished inside a heated building. Additionally, the pelvic bone plus a complete leg bone, front and back, had to be cleaned and shipped with the hide to assist in building the body mold. The meat was then distributed to the needy families in the village. One of the families invited me to dinner, and I tasted my first musk-ox meat. It was excellent. The hides, skull and bones were boxed and shipped according to instructions and six months later the completed specimen was on display beside the buffalo.

Other smaller animals and birds were taken for museums and universities in the course of my tour of duty. Geese and ducks were collected from different parts of the Territory to help determine the range of species and sub-species. Many of these were skinned and preserved for easier shipping. Diseased animals such as rabid fox were killed in areas where there was concern for the welfare of the people living in close proximity. The heads of the animals had to be removed while I wore rubber gloves, and shipped to laboratories for examination. Not a pleasant job, especially knowing that any saliva getting into a cut could result in death.

All things considered and being a hunter by nature, I felt that this part of the job had its compensations. No one likes to see wildlife suffer and being in a position to put crippled animals out of their misery had its rewards. It was never pleasant having to kill and remove animals because they did not fit in man's environment, but it was and is an unavoidable fact of life and someone had to do it. There is no such thing as the utopian balance of nature as preached by some, and as long as man and wildlife must co-exist it will have to be by man's standards. To believe otherwise is to foster mass losses of wildlife to starvation and disease, which is difficult to support. Removing surplus stocks by sound management and controlled killing is as necessary as stocking depleted populations. ■

Chapter 15

Arctic Survey

Each YEAR IN LATE APRIL agents from the Fairbanks office made a patrol of the Native villages in arctic Alaska to survey the economy of the villages and the utilization of wildlife. Emphasis was placed on the caribou take. At the same time the locations and movement of caribou herds were noted and all wildlife observed were recorded on maps for the management biologists.

One of the first of these arctic surveys was conducted by Ray Woolford, enforcement chief of the northern district, and I in 1954. It was on this trip that I ran the Gullwing Stinson up into the bushes on the lake behind Kobuk as related in an earlier chapter. I also flew the surveys in 1957 and 1958, even though I was stationed in McGrath, because of the experience I had gained in the earlier patrols. Most of the information that follows has been extracted from the three reports written at the completion of the surveys.

Upon arriving at a village, our first contact was generally with the teachers or traders. We explained that we were gathering data on the village economy and that we were attempting to obtain an accurate estimate of the number of caribou killed by the villagers during the past year. We tried to make it clear that our visit was a fact-finding mission, that information we obtained would not be used in a retaliatory manner. In organized villages all of our discussions were held with members of the Native council. The game regulations were explained in detail, as were the various activities of the service. The wolf control program and the arctic game survey were highlighted.

Fortunately, our visits in 1954 coincided with that year's

game survey, and many of the people had seen the Beechcraft as it flew over their village. As a result of the arctic game survey and wolf control program, we were able to tell the groups that the caribou bag limit had been raised from three to five.

The information contained in these reports was based entirely upon personal interviews with village council leaders, teachers and traders. Completeness of the information was directly proportional to the interest shown by village leaders.

To illustrate the depth of this survey I have extracted the section on the village of Shungnak from Ray Woolford's 1954 report entitled "Notes on Village Economies and Wildlife Utilization in Arctic Alaska."

Shungnak

Along a sidehill bordering the north bank of the river, 12 miles downstream from Kobuk, lies the village of Shungnak with a total population of 142 Eskimos and 150 dogs. There are 42 families with 45 children under 6 years of age, 33 children of school age, and the remainder of the people are older than 18 years of age. According to local sources, the population is slowly but steadily increasing.

The Shungnak school is staffed and operated by the Alaska Native Service. The building is of frame construction and contains more than one classroom. The Friends denomination, supervised by a Mr. Beck of Kotzebue, maintains a church in this village. The religious services are conducted by a local Native minister.

Local village government is very highly organized in Shungnak. There are two councils: One acts as the village governing authority; the efforts of the other are devoted primarily to the management of the cooperative store. According to Mr. Graham, ANS teacher, these groups are self-sufficient, and very rarely is it necessary to call for the assistance of a deputy marshal. On the 27th of December each year an election is held at which time three new council members are elected. Residents of Shungnak are definitely opposed to the establishment of a reservation and so expressed themselves in the plebiscite of 1950.

Inbound freight from Seattle to Shungnak is carried aboard the ANS North Star. At Kotzebue it is lightered to river boats and barges and taken upstream to Shungnak. Both river and air freight costs are identical to those previously indicated for the village of Kobuk. Wien Alaska Airlines bush planes land at

Shungnak twice weekly carrying mail, passengers and freight. The ANS school is equipped with a functioning two-way radio telephone with a direct tie-in with the ANS Hospital and the Alaska Communications System at Kotzebue.

The Shungnak Native Store is a village cooperative managed by an elected council. According to the council, it operates upon a strictly cash basis. It is not, however, patronized exclusively by all residents, as the privately operated store at Kobuk does considerable business with its downriver neighbors. Costs of the eight basic food items per pound at the Shungnak store are:

Flour, 50 lbs.	— $7.50	Lard, 4 lbs.	— $ 1.25
Sugar, 50 lbs.	— $ .20	Rolled oats, 9 lbs.	— $ 1.80
Tea, 50 lbs.	— $1.70	Corn meal, 10 lbs.	— $ 2.00
Coffee, 50 lbs.	— $1.25	Canned milk, case	— $11.00

The possibilities of local employment and industry at Shungnak are very promising. An unlimited supply of the gem stone, jade, is found along the nearby Shungnak River. Elaborate equipment for cutting and polishing of stones has been arranged in assembly line position in the school basement. Three complete machines, including the tools and templates for the manufacturing of jewelry have been provided. The jade project presently employs three adults and five to six school age children. Considering the time involved in the manufactured products, employees engaged at this labor earn approximately $1.45 per hour. During the past two years a community income of $5,000 has been derived from the manufacture and sale of jade products. Another means of revenue for the people of Shungnak have been the sewing of mukluks and parkas and the construction of birch bark baskets. Sales of these products average about $750 annually.

From five to seven men fly to Fairbanks each spring where they are employed during a four month period of seasonal employment. During this time their earnings range from $1,500 to $2,200. Of these amounts various percentages return to the village. One or two outstanding individuals will return with all their summer salary minus expenses; one or two will return with an empty pocketbook and an appetite; while others may return with from $300 to $500. It appears to be almost impossible to arrive at a percentage of outside earned income returning to the village.

More easily identified are the sources of "Unearned Income."

For Shungnak last year these were as listed:

No.	Source	Month	Year
6	Old Age Pensions	$270.00	$ 3,240
?	Unemployment Comp.	—	1,308*
10	Aid to Dependent Children	$500.00	6,000
?	Army Dependents	$ 91.30	1,095
		Total	$11,643

Unemployment compensation figures are totals for months of February and April. Data in this category for other months were not available.

The annual per capita income unearned is $82.00, while the average per family is $277.23.

During the past year the caribou migration, fortunately or unfortunately, depending upon the outlook, did not swing close to Shungnak. The nearest crossing was at least 30 miles west of the village. Reports indicate the rabbit population is increasing. Fur bearing animals that are available to Shungnak trappers are muskrat, mink, otter, fox, weasel, beaver and lynx. During the summer months salmon, whitefish, and pike are caught with seines and gill nets. No figures were obtained relative to the take of the several species of fish. Council members stated, however, that when the fish runs failed to materialize it became necessary to kill caribou for summer food. It was also mentioned that, "Some families don't fish, then have hard luck." No gardening is attempted in Shungnak. It is possible and was rather extensively practiced several years ago. The reason for the present lack of gardening is the movement of the people away from the village to their fish camps.

An examination of the fur records of the Native store along with questioning of several council members and the ANS teacher indicated the following listed take of game and fur animals:

Caribou — 250 Mink — 30 Otter — 2
Weasel — 13 Red Fox — 7 Wolves — 10

In a discussion regarding the actual number of caribou required as food by the Natives of Shungnak, council members stated that two caribou for each adult and one for each child would be sufficient, provided fishing was normal. With a poor fishing season it would become necessary to kill more caribou. Village and store council members present at the time this information was obtained were Charlie Lee, James Commack, Gene Lee and Charlie Douglas. Also attending the discussion was ANS teacher Mr. Graham.

Once during the trip we were able to learn of the reaction to our questioning. Louie Rotman of Kotzebue provided us with a copy of the letter below which he had received just after our visit to Selawik. Louie owned the largest store and roadhouse in Kotzebue and stores in several outlying villages. These were operated by Natives. We delivered two rifles to the store at the request of Mr. Rotman.

Selawik, Alaska
May 6, 1954

Louis Rotman
Dear Friend—
    I received two .22 rifle yesterday by Fish & Wildlife Service. Some people brings a words from Kiana and Noorvik lots of Indians going to come down to look for young men and young ladies to kill some. So some people afraid to go up the river. Paul Stanley brings down his stuff to village. Oh foolish I told them we have government a strong law, no killing anybodys too bad, Here is two small checks $27.92. Yes if clara up to her if she like to come as last spring. Hope people will get lots of rats. But seems no water again. This game warden asking too many things even, they asking the price grube & they dont talk much Nelson Walker. Well Not Much to write,

Your Friend
(signed by the manager of the Selawik store)

Nelson Walker was a bush pilot from Kotzebue who also owned a store in the village.

This was a most interesting letter because it focused on the deep rooted fear that still existed between the Eskimos and Indians. Small wars had been fought between these two cultures for centuries, and small skirmishes continued up into the late 1800s and early 1900s. It was common for the winning side to take some of the women as captives, forcing them to carry plunder back to the home village. Because of the distances involved in carrying out these battles there was never a total victory, and the losers always planned retaliation. This kept both sides in discomposure, especially in the fall as darkness set in, making villages more susceptible to a sneak attack. Any bad omen such as an unexplained dream, unusual animal behavior or meterological disturbance was enough to throw the community into frantic behavior. The men would not travel to hunt or trap, and if there was not an adequate supply of food on hand the people suffered.

When we landed on the river ice at the village of Selawik we were surprised at the number of people who lined the bank to check us out. Kotzebue had been our base of operation for several days as we visited the surrounding villages. We stayed at Rotman's Hotel, and in the evenings Louie had briefed us on what to expect and who to contact in the different communities. He had said that most of the men at Selawik were out muskrat hunting. This was the backbone of the local economy — the area was surrounded by lakes that produced the finest quality skins in Alaska. It was also one of the most pleasurable times of the year as the long spring days warmed up the Arctic.

We were therefore very surprised to see so many young men sitting idly around the village and asked the storekeeper for an explanation. He indicated that they were all concerned with the rumor that Indians from the Koyukuk were enroute to raid the village and steal the women. At the time of our arrival the rumor had grown significantly, and the word was that the villages of Noorvik and Kiana had already been pillaged. This was difficult to believe. We would have considered it a ploy for welfare purposes except that the trappers looked forward to the hunt not only for muskrats but for the ducks and geese that were arriving. After a long discussion with the storekeeper we suggested that he advise the men that there was no substance to the rumor. We had visited both Noorvik and Kiana within the past few days and assured him that all was well. Further, we had recently been sealing beaver skins in Indian villages along the Koyukuk and could testify that there were no preparations being made for war. He appreciated the information and decided to pass it on immediately before the entire season was lost. Apparently it worked because we found out later that many of the hunters went to their camps and resumed normal activities.

When we reported this information to Louie that night he was visibly upset because most of the villages had large debts at the store, and he had extended additional credit to outfit the hunters for the spring season. He appreciated our efforts and hoped for the best. The letter from Rotman's storekeeper arrived the next day.

The next village we visited was Kobuk. This was the home of Harry Brown, one of the five members of the Alaska Game Commission. Harry had lived in the country since the turn of the century, had married an Eskimo woman and opened a store in Kobuk sometime in the 1920s. His daughter May was married to Tony Bernhardt, and together they were now running the store

for Harry, who considered himself retired. During lunch we told them about the Selawik incident. Harry scoffed, but May, who was born and raised in Kobuk, did not appear amused. The village of Kobuk was the closest Eskimo village to any of the Indian communities. It was along the route of the overland pass from the Koyukuk to the Kobuk River by way of the Hog and Pah River portage. According to May, the people of this small settlement became fearful in the fall and were ready for immediate flight should the Indians make an appearance. We jokingly asked what would happen if we picked up some old

Indian moccasins and other paraphernalia and secretly scattered them around the woods close to the dog team trails where they would be found. Without smiling and very seriously she said that everyone in the village would flee, including herself. We decided that our sense of humor was not well appreciated and decided not to pursue our game any further. The fear was deeply ingrained, and even though we felt it was hard to believe in this day and age, we had not been raised in this culture and could not appreciate the depths of their beliefs.

We did understand, however, their need for wildlife and questioned them diligently on the different methods used for taking game and the amount of game needed to support a family. We also asked about the kinds of wildlife used to feed sled dogs, and the villagers' knowledge of animals and fish populations. Also recorded were their observations of the effects of weather and predation on wildlife populations. The following are excerpts from the 1954 report.

It is interesting to note that in every village, except Barrow, the number of dogs exceeds the number of humans. During the decade of the oil exploration at Barrow, the dogs were not nearly so necessary to the village economy. The pursuit of white foxes and food animals gave way to the wage earners and store foods. Now being faced with the necessity of returning partially to the old way of life, dogs are regaining their former position in the Barrow economy, and in a short time their numbers will exceed the humans, as in other villages. A high percentage of the wildlife utilized by the Natives of northern Alaska is consumed as dog food. It is very likely that the identical economic level of a family or village could be maintained with fewer of the beasts. However, in Native life, dog ownership is a matter of prestige. The more dogs a man owns, the higher is his standing in the community.

None of the game animals are easy for Selawik residents to obtain. Caribou usually range no closer than 50 miles to the village. Rabbits are very scarce. Ptarmigan are plentiful during the winter months, and ducks and geese are plentiful during the period of open water. Mink and muskrat are the two most valuable fur bearers sought by local trappers. Whitefish, sheefish and pike are available the year-round and accordingly, fish play a predominant part in the local diet. Salmon are not available to the people of Selawik, "Maybe we get one or two, three sometimes, maybe four."

The take of fur and game animals at Selawik was determined to be as follows:

Caribou — 150   Mink — 406   Muskrat — 13,000

One "crazy acting" fox was killed in the village during April 1954.

Eskimo William Sheldon said that for his family and dogs he needed a total of 10 caribou a month. In figuring food requirements for his dogs, he said that a team averaging nine dogs would require three caribou a month, provided all parts including the guts were used.

The only big game animal available in numbers to the people of Noorvik is the wandering caribou. A migration of caribou appeared in the hills east of Noorvik during September 1953 and stragglers were still observed in the area in early May 1954. Rabbits are on the increase, and ptarmigan are reported to be abundant. An occasional moose wanders down the Kobuk as far as Noorvik. If sighted, his travels are over. Two moose, a male and a female, were shot at Noorvik within recent months.

The chief fur producing animals of the area are mink and muskrat. Mink were numerous during the last open season but the catch was somewhat less than usual. An all Alaska National Guard encampment was held at Anchorage during the middle of the trapping season, thus removing most of the young, more energetic trappers from the tundra. Local residents have complained that winter grazing of reindeer in the area west of Noorvik has contributed to the decline of the muskrats. "The reindeer, he trample and paw pushup. Muskrat freeze." As near as could be determined from local sources of information, the take of game and fur animals for Noorvik was as follows:

Caribou — 200   Mink — 308   Muskrat —5,600

A Selawik trapper stated "East wind, warm up, muskrat come out. West wind start to blow, freeze-up, muskrat go inside. Warm up then not many come out."

The only Natives in Alaska almost totally dependent upon a single game animal are the Eskimos of Anaktuvuk Pass. Caribou are essential to their existence. Their food is the meat of the caribou. Their winter clothing is made from the hide of the caribou. Their tents, stretched over a willow or alder framework, are caribou skins sewn together. If the caribou fails to appear in Anaktuvuk Pass, Eskimos must leave the village and travel until the animal is found.

At the north end of the pass the Eskimos have erected a caribou lead. Starting on the mountain side to the east, it runs across the valley for a distance of about three miles. Long pieces of sod chopped from the ground or piles of rocks were erected at intervals in a straight line. Bits of cloth fastened to the tops of the sod or rock piles wave in the breeze. Caribou, approaching along a natural migration route from the east, follow the "fence" to its end, then turn south. Here Natives lie in waiting and the animals are taken.

With the caribou are the wolves. Bounty money, paid by the Territory, is the chief source of income directly related to the wildlife resource. At Anaktuvuk Pass this was estimated to have been $3,330 from wolves and wolverine during the past year — $256.15 per family or $44.40 per individual.

The take of fur and game animals, as estimated by Homer Mekiana of Anaktuvuk Pass, during the past year is:

Fox	— 150	Wolverine	— 12
Ermine	— 30	Wolves	— 63
Caribou	— 2,000		

The following table has been prepared to show the estimated take of caribou by the twelve villages visited during the spring of 1954. All figures are for the year immediately preceding the date of the visit.

Estimated Caribou Take

Village	Number of Caribou
Kobuk	25
Shungnak	250
Kiana	800
Noorvik	200
Selawik	150
Noatak	750
Kotzebue	1,000
Kivalina	500

Village	Number of Caribou
Point Lay	*500*
Wainwright	*1,000*
Point Barrow	*2,000*
Anaktuvuk Pass	*2,000*
Total	9,175

The above estimates were obtained by questioning members of the various Native councils, traders and teachers. Doubtless the estimates are low, for caribou provide one of the principal sources of food in each village. The people are afraid to accurately report their take, if they actually remember the numbers they have killed, for fear of retaliation or subsequent restrictions on the part of the Fish and Wildlife Service. No estimate was obtained from the small settlements along the coast east of Barrow nor from Barter Island.

Whenever caribou are available, as many as possible are killed. No effort is made to dispatch wounded animals which escape. Herd shooting is a general practice, and, thus, many of the animals drop far from the scene of the shooting.

Information obtained in several of the villages with regard to the caribou requirements of the people supports the contention that the take estimates are low. At Anaktuvuk Pass for instance the estimated take was 2,000 animals, a figure mutually agreed upon by trader O'Connel and Postmaster Mekiana. The people of Anaktuvuk exist primarily upon caribou. O'Connel stated the village dogs were fed almost exclusively on caribou and that a team of seven dogs requires one animal each week. Mekiana stated that when eating nothing but meat, his family totaling nine of various ages needed one caribou each day. By using these statements to compute the village take, the original estimate jumps alarmingly.

52 caribou a year for 7 dogs
17.7 teams of 7 dogs each at Anaktuvuk
17.7 x 52 . . . .   920.4
and
1 caribou a day per family of 9
8.3 families of 9 in population
8.3 x 365 . . . . 3,029.5
Total   3,949.9
It is quite probable that the 4,000 figure more accurately

describes the Anaktuvuk caribou take, and it is equally probable the remaining village estimates could be revised upwards.

The Eskimos will kill caribou without regard to the legal bag limit as long as the animals are available. Considering the periods of accessibility to the villages visited, the take during the past year is estimated by the writer to have been at least 15,000 animals.

SUMMARY

In each of the 12 villages previously described the population is increasing. This trend will likely continue and is attributable, in part at least, to the advancement of the educational, health and welfare programs. The table following shows the 1954 populations, numbers of families and numbers of dogs in each village. The 1980 census figures are added for comparison purposes.

Populations

Village	Population 1954	1980	Families	Dogs	Dogs Per Capita	Per Family
Kobuk	53	64	9	105	1.98	11.6
Shungnak	142	208	42	150	1.05	3.5
Kiana	178	356	44	400	2.24	9.0
Noorvik	300	508	64	500	1.66	7.8
Selawik	300	372	52	600	2.00	11.5
Noatak	290	273	45	400	1.37	8.8
Kotzebue	820	2,250	—	1,000	1.02	—
Kivalina	132	249	24	150	1.13	6.2
Point Lay	66	68	12	100	1.51	8.3
Wainwright	225	410	41	350	1.55	8.5
Point Barrow	1,200	2,539	175	1,000	.83	5.8
Anaktuvuk	75	235	13	124	1.66	9.6
Totals	3,781	7,532	521*	4,879	1.29	7.4*

* Does not include Kotzebue

There has been some noticeable changes in the population trends of the arctic villages as shown in the 1980 census figures. The most significant is a shift of people out of the bush villages into the large communities of Kotzebue and Point Barrow. A different lifestyle has emerged, causing new problems and concerns among Native leaders in the meshing of old ways with the new. Gone for the most part is the need for the true subsistence way of life, although many of the older people still cling proudly to the old culture and consequently are having a great deal of difficulty accepting the new society. All of the major problems connected with drug and alcohol abuse are now found in the villages. The state has police trained Village Public Safety Officers in most of the settlements and the state troopers are constantly having to respond to reports of violent crimes much the same as in the bigger cities. All of this is a far cry from 30 years ago when the problems were mostly minor and could be handled by the village councils with only occasional help from U.S. Marshals.

The villages themselves have also changed dramatically. Dog teams have been replaced for the most part by snowmachines, TV antennas adorn houses, telephone and power lines run from house to house, and even outhouses are disappearing. Modern schools have large gyms, and basketball teams travel to compete with other schools via a vast network of air transportation that links communities as effectively as the road systems of the Lower 48.

All this modernization has not only changed the social structures of the villages, it's made a new impact on the wildlife, and game managers are having difficulty keeping up. While on the one hand a subsistence take is necessary to a certain extent for some, it is not as compelling as many leaders indicate. The biggest problem is the selling of wildlife and parts by some to support a dependency on alcohol and drugs. In the last big ivory bust, which netted several dealers and suppliers for possession of illegal walrus tusks, I was advised by my former colleagues that the suppliers were most interested in trying to make deals with the undercover agent for a trade in drugs, mostly cocaine. Some fish buyers along the Yukon River trade marijuana for fish eggs, and we have dope and alcohol dealers flying around in private aircraft making all sorts of deals for wildlife products.

This puts a new dimension on resource management, one that cannot be taken lightly. Congress has provided special provisions for Natives to take marine mammals for traditional use. I'm sure no one considers the taking of these mammals as barter for drugs a traditional use, but enforcement agencies are left to prosecute violations which become emotional and entangled with those seeking to continue a true subsistence lifestyle. The job confronting enforcement agents today is complex, and most often not supported by those responsible for enacting laws which either cannot be enforced or make a mockery of wildlife conservation and management. They face a constant uphill battle that promises to become more complicated and lonely in the years ahead until laws and regulations are based on reality and not on radical emotions. ■

Chapter 16

Search
and Rescue

ONE PHASE OF OUR JOB that was never detailed in manuals or policy was search and rescue work. It was not the responsibility of the Fish and Wildlife Service to search for missing planes, boats or persons, but because of the size and remoteness of the Territory, we reacted to local calls for assistance without hesitation. The unwritten policy allowed us this prerogative, but if a search went on for a long while we had to back off and let the military take control. Then we assisted only when authorized by headquarters.

At the McGrath headquarters appeals for help were relayed by radio and usually involved someone overdue from a trip. We were requested to check the route of travel. If it was a missing plane the Civil Aviation Administration, forerunner of the present FAA, was usually involved and would have either flight plan information or knowledge about the pilot's flying habits if he was a local. In the event a boat or dog team was missing — there were no snow machines in those days — the information was relayed by concerned families or friends. Bush pilots and private pilots donated their time without hesitation, knowing full well they could be the object of the next search. This alliance gave pilots a comforting feeling. It was nice knowing that if you had to make an emergency landing, someone would be looking as soon as the alarm was sent out.

Sometimes the search involved friends and became very personal such as the time in 1958 when Paul Tovey and Phil Pentacost, two school teacher acquaintances, were overdue on a short trip with Paul's plane. They had departed the village of Minto during the Christmas holidays for a day of wolf hunting and had not returned. Phil's wife Dorothy sent out the alarm with a request for an immediate search because of the severe cold weather that prevailed at the time. I was briefed at the McGrath CAA flight service station and told that Dorothy Pentacost had indicated that they had planned to hunt the Kantishna River country. I was familiar with the area and advised the coordinators that I would land and check with the trappers to determine if they had seen the plane.

Paul Tovey had worked a few years for the Fish and Wildlife Service as a biologist. The Pentacosts were close friends, and I had spent many enjoyable evenings with them at their home when they were teaching at Tuluksak, a village on the lower Kuskokwim River. Phil was an avid hunter, and we talked many times into the wee hours about rifles and bullet velocities. I knew they were both capable of taking care of themselves in the wilderness; however, if they were hurt, it would be difficult at best to survive in the extreme cold that prevailed.

My field diary indicates that I departed from McGrath on the morning of December 29 with the temperature registering -42° and only one magneto firing on the Cessna 180 engine. Normally I would never have contemplated a trip in that temperature with a faulty ignition system. However, friends' lives were at stake. I searched the Kantishna and Toklat River areas and landed at several trapline camps to talk with the trappers. They had not seen nor heard any aircraft flying around during the previous four days. The cold spell had them holed up at their main camps and with noise carrying greater distances in the cold air, they felt they would have heard any aircraft engine cruising the area. They each had heard my Cessna for several minutes before I came into view. With darkness arriving by 3:00 p.m. in the short days of December, I went on to Fairbanks and had a mechanic work on the magneto.

The next morning I was off again with the temperature at -46°, but this time the ignition system was working properly. I searched areas which according to headquarters had not yet been covered. This included the watersheds of the Totaklanika and Toklat rivers to the headwaters, then back to the Moose River, Birch Creek, McKinley Fork and Lake Minchumina. I landed and talked with several more trappers who each indicated that on the days in question it had been snowing with low ceilings and not suitable for flying in that part of the country. This information was passed on to the control center and the area eliminated from the search plan. I returned to McGrath.

The weather got colder and the only searching accomplished was at night by the military with large aircraft looking for camp fires. I was very upset at not being allowed to participate, but policy dictated no flying at below -50°. Rumors abounded and I remember going into depression on New Year's Eve when one of the CAA communicators mentioned that he heard their frozen bodies had been found in a cabin on the Kantishna. That was my search area, and I felt completely let down, thinking that I must have missed seeing evidence of them that might have saved their lives. The information was wrong, however, but I kept having a nagging feeling that I missed them somewhere, somehow. After the weather moderated it got nasty with heavy snow for several days, eliminating any search efforts. Everyone knew the chances of finding them alive now were remote. The search continued for several weeks, and I covered the Nowitna River watersheds, locating several big bands of wolves, but no aircraft. Finally the remnants of their aircraft were found. It had crashed and burned just a few miles from Minto. They had been killed on impact. It was a sad day, but at least their bodies were found and the matter laid to rest.

There are times however, when lost planes are not found, causing added grief to friends and relatives when the fate of their loved ones is unknown. Such was the case of my brother-in-law Johnny Sommer. In November 1954 he flew his Piper Pacer from Nulato to Koyukuk and then departed late in the evening for Ruby, a distance of only 45 miles. Accompanying him was his friend Philip Hundorf who was getting married the next day. They never arrived at Ruby.

We conducted a search effort that lasted for more than a week and were unsuccessful at locating any clues to the fate of the two men. Both were experienced woodsmen, having lived all their lives along the Yukon River, and we knew that if they had survived a crash they would endure for a long time, even though the temperature was below zero. Based on this, the search effort ranged well beyond what would have been a straight line flight between the two villages, all to no avail. The conclusion: They were forced down onto the river ice and disappeared through one of the many sections that had not completely frozen.

John Sommer, Johnny's dad and my father-in-law, was more than 80 at the time and could never accept the fact that his son was gone. Neither could his wife Agnes nor the rest of the family. Had the two men been found and put to rest the family would have been at ease; however, there was always the nagging feeling that they had survived and were suffering somewhere in the wilderness. John passed away never knowing what had happened to his son, although it was a constantly vexing source of grief to him.

Five years later the pilot of a small plane approaching Galena caught a glint of metal reflecting from the sun in the thick timber not far from the runway. A search party went out and located the wreckage of Johnny's plane. It was on a direct line from Koyukuk to Ruby, completely hidden by dense spruce trees. Why it crashed no one will ever know, but the tragedy was compounded by the heavy timber that closed in over the demolished aircraft and concealed the men's fate, giving no peace nor rest to the families until many years later.

There was also the famous search for Clarence Rhode, the regional director of the U.S. Fish and Wildlife Service, his son Jack, and Stan Frederickson, a game management agent from Fairbanks. Little did I realize when I received the fateful message at McGrath on August 23, 1958, telling me to proceed north and look for Grumman N720 piloted by Rhode that I would be on a search that would last past freeze up. For the first few days there were just a few of us with Fish and Wildlife Service aircraft checking the areas in the remote Brooks Range where Rhode had planned to operate. Clarence and Stan were on a reconnaissance sheep patrol operating out of Porcupine Lake and were to return to Fairbanks on August 22. The weather had been bad and radio signals nonexistent. On the 25th the search efforts were put under the direction of the military search and rescue group. The northern half of Alaska was sectioned off into numbered grids and we were assigned specific search areas each day. As many as 28 planes were involved during the first few weeks searching an area of over 280,000 square miles (about twice the area of California). More than 2,000 flying hours were totaled up, with 260 people involved, all to no avail.

For my part it was a frustrating effort with many tight jawed turns in fog-shrouded canyons trying to check every nook and cranny that might conceal a black and orange Grumman. This was the chief that was missing, along with a fellow agent and a young college student who had but six hours of course work to complete before receiving a degree. Each day we started out full of enthusiasm, especially if the weather was good, which it was not often, thinking that this was the day they would be found. After several weeks, however, we all knew the chances of finding them alive became remote as we began covering many of the prime areas for the third and fourth time.

The next summer we conducted another search from Chandler Lake with several float aircraft. This was terminated when one of the search planes was reported missing in the eastern section of the Brooks Range. Another all-out search was started which lasted for seven or eight days. The plane, a Cessna 180, was located in a valley on Mount Davidson where it had crashed making a tight uphill turn in weather. Both the pilot and passenger survived. They were weary from living in wet sleeping bags and being plagued by mosquitoes but alive and happy to be rescued.

That ended the official search for N720. However, most aircraft and helicopters pilots flying in the area during the next few years kept an eye open for the missing amphibian. Everyone involved had a theory on what happened. Many felt he had made a hard landing, or wheels-down landing on a lake and had sunk. Others theorized that the extra fuel he was carrying in cans exploded in flight, disintegrating the aircraft. Others, including myself, felt that the plane had hit the side of a hill or mountain, scattering the plane in bits and pieces over the countryside.

It wasn't until 21 years later that the mystery was solved. On August 23, 1979, two women hikers traversing a 5,700 foot pass at the head of the Ivishak River spotted the wreckage of an aircraft. At first they thought the patch of orange was lichen contrasted against the dark grays of the ridge. A closer look revealed an airplane smashed against the mountainside. They found significant evidence including the flight logs that were turned over to the National Transportation Safety Board. An investigator sent to the scene identified the plane as the missing N720, thus ending the mystery of our missing leader's fate.

How many patches of orange lichen or dwarf birch with orange and red fall colors I checked during the search I'll never know, but it was a considerable number. Each time we spotted the colors in a valley, on a ridge or against a canyon wall my pulse would quicken as I thought it might be the plane, and slow in relief when it wasn't.

Why we didn't find the plane during the most intensive search in Alaska's history has been the topic of many discussions since the wreck was found. It was within short distance of Porcupine Lake where they had planned to operate, and at the head of a logical pass leading back toward Fairbanks. One good reason was that it was probably covered with a skiff of snow shortly after the crash. Also, the wreckage was scattered in small pieces over a rock and shale formation, making it extremely difficult to see. When the NTSB inspectors went to the crash site by helicopter with the girl who found the plane as a guide, they had difficulty locating the wreckage from the air even though she knew the exact location. Under these circumstances it would have been a chance sighting at best, and unfortunately no search plane happened over the right spot at the right time with the proper reflective angle of light necessary to spot one of the small pieces of metal laying in the rocks.

Clarence's wife died in 1971 without knowing what happened to her husband. According to Jim Rhode, the youngest member of the family, his mother used to have recurring dreams about seeing his dad and brother alive. In her dreams they were sitting on a rocky hillside with the plane wreckage in the background. "Where have you been Clarence?" his wife would ask. "I'll tell you later," he would reply. "How are the kids?"

Occasionally we were involved in a search that not only had a happy ending but provided some humor as well. One that had an interesting ending occurred at the village of Old Crow, Yukon Territory, Canada. Fred Woldstad, chief of the State Fish and Wildlife Protection Division, and I went to Old Crow in January 1961 to fly a joint patrol of the Canadian-Alaskan boundary with the Royal Canadian Mounted Police. We had a mutual problem of trappers crossing the border back and forth and hunting and trapping in violation of the laws of the two countries. The day after we arrived the temperature plummeted to -50°, and a dense ice fog covered the valley preventing any flying. Staffing the post were constables Jim Lambert and Duane Crosland who proved to be very gracious hosts and provided us with many interesting insights into the problems of policing this section of the Arctic.

They were still using dog teams to patrol the district, which included the villages of Fort McPherson, Arctic Red River and Hershel Island on the coast and all the country between. The previous year Constable Lambert made a patrol from Old Crow to Fort McPherson, Arctic Red, Inuvik, Aklavik, Hershel Island and back, logging more than 800 miles in 19 days. When he was stationed at Hershel Island he traveled more than 5,000 miles a year with dogs.

At the time, Old Crow and the other villages were dry, meaning liquor could not legally be sold or brought into town. The police kept a tight reign on the consumption of alcoholic beverages, and consequently there were few serious problems, which was very refreshing after seeing the degradation that was occurring in our Alaska villages.

The ice fog dissipated on the third day even though the temperature still remained in the -40 degrees. Jim Lambert approached us at breakfast with a request to conduct a search. One of the Native women in the village was concerned about her husband who was away trapping on the Whitestone River. According to Jim, around Christmas she had found dead mice in her cabin — an ominous sign, which, according to the Athabaskan belief, indicated that someone in her immediate family had died.

It was the responsibility of the RCMP to respond to these requests whenever possible, and if our plane was available, he would check out the situation for the worried woman. We agreed and prepared the aircraft for departure.

Jim arrived with his survival gear and the village chief, Charlie Peter, acting as guide because he knew the location of the trapline in question. After takeoff from the ski strip on the river, we climbed to 5,000 feet and found a temperature inversion with warmer air to fly in. It took about an hour to fly to the main trapline cabin located on a bank of the river. We could see dog team trails leading in several directions but no signs of life at the cabin. The dogs and sled were gone, indicating that our trapper was traveling. I decided to make a low pass to determine the feasibililty of landing on the river and to determine which trail was the most recently used so we could follow it in the direction he was traveling.

As we descended in slow flight to tree top level we immediately learned two things: The snow was too deep to take off from the narrow river; and, it was dang cold. I eased the power back on and the engine balked momentarily from the super cold air running through the carburetor. We had to follow a few bends until we had full power again and were able to climb into the warmer air. Looking back after we gained altitude we could see a vapor trail — left by our airplane — over that part of the river we had just flown. The temperature had to be in the -60 degrees down there — not a place to land for sure. Later, when we were discussing the flight back at the barracks, Jim Lambert indicated he had become quite shook when the engine coughed, and he figured we were going in. He was more than happy to give up any thoughts of landing.

We followed the most recent dog team trail across open meadows, along sloughs, and through spruce thickets in an easterly direction for about 45 miles. It ended up at the mess wanigan of an oil exploration party that was proceeding north with five tractors and sleds. The dog team was tied up outside and the trapper was obviously inside enjoying a warm meal and companionship. We flew back to Old Crow to report our findings to the trapper's wife, knowing she would have mixed emotions about our findings and the fact that the dead mice had lied. The search was recorded in the journals of the RCMP as another successful episode in the annals of the famed northern police organization.

There was the interesting search and rescue of the mysterious Richard Hartley in August 1959. I was in my McGrath office on April 14 doing beaver sealing reports when one of the local bush pilots advised me that he had just completed a flight to the upper Big River and dropped off an outsider who, with his meager outfit, planned to prospect that area. He told the pilot he planned to build a raft after breakup and float down to McGrath. We wondered if the man had enough supplies, so I checked with the clerk at the Northern Commercial Company who listed the supplies he had purchased as:

8 lbs. beans	1 lb. rice
3 lbs. dried apples	1 lb. salt
2 lbs. sugar	1 can pepper
3 lbs. crisco	1 lb. tea
1 lb. margarine	Assorted candy bars

Since he was camped in good mountain sheep country I thought it wise to contact and advise Hartley that the hunting season was closed and that it would not be legal for him to kill game to add to his meager food supplies.

On April 20 I landed at Hartley's camp. He was living under a small tarp, and his cooking kit consisted of a small frying pan and pot. The snow was three feet deep, and, having no snowshoes, he could not extend his trails more than a few hundred yards of the camp. After introducing myself and advising him about the game laws, he said he was aware that he could not legally shoot game, but he was not worried. He had camped a few winters in the Black Hills of North Dakota with limited supplies and felt he would make out okay. Hartley did admit, however, that he had not counted on the snow being so deep or the weather being so cold. I asked if he was familiar with mountain rivers in the spring, and he said no.

I decided he could not make it here until breakup and, because he would not consider returning to McGrath, I moved him downstream about eight miles to an unused cabin that would afford shelter from the heavy winds and rains. I estimated his total outfit, including food, rifle, ax, swede saw and sleeping bag, to weigh approximately 60 pounds. He was wearing a wool jacket, ski cap, wool pants and shoe pacs. Temperatures had been recorded down to -20° during the night at Farewell, about 60 miles away.

By May 28 no one had heard or seen Hartley, so a trip was made to the cabin on Big River to see how he was doing. Because the plane was now on floats and the river at that location unsuitable for a landing, the cabin was checked from the air.

Sig Olson
'61

It appeared to be vacant so I flew the full length of the river to its mouth on the Kuskokwim and then downstream to McGrath. There was no trace of the fellow.

On June 6 Hartley still had not shown up, so I made another trip up Big River, this time with Len Jones, the weather bureau station manager at McGrath, as observer. There was no sign of Hartley on the way up, but on the way back we saw him waving frantically from a sand bar where he had stamped out the word HELP. We made a difficult landing in the narrow, swift glacier river choked with debris and fallen trees.

Hartley was hardly recognizable from weight loss. His clothes were torn, and his shoe pacs were worn through. His rifle was all that remained from his outfit. He said he had lost three rafts and for six days had been making slow progress walking the game trails along the river bank through dense growths of willow and spruce. Without insect repellent, he had been plagued by mosquitoes and was a mass of bites and sores. The only food he had eaten for more than two weeks were two squirrels which he had shot and cooked on a stick. He told us that he had abandoned hope of walking to any settlement. As we flew back to McGrath over the route he was trying to follow we realized that, indeed, he could not have made it. After we landed he said thanks and took off for the Northern Commercial Company.

Later the clerk told me that as Hartley was buying a new outfit of clothes he kept remarking that he was happy to be alive and pleased because he found what he had gone out for. No one knew what that was, and to my knowledge he has never returned. He was one of the lucky ones, though. Many newcomers disappeared and were never found again. Others we found, but only after it was too late, when all we could do was ship the bodies back to the families.

For my efforts in the Hartley episode I received the Department of Interior's valor award. As the commendation was being read at the department's award ceremony in Washington, D.C., I could not help but think how closely related the circumstances are that make you either a hero or a failure. Had I wrecked the aircraft during my search, I would have received a different award, but because I was successful, I enjoyed a bit of recognition. I'm convinced everything in life is connected to timing, and in this case, my timing was right and so was Hartley's. ■

Chapter 17

Enforcement Agents and Biologists

IT'S NO SECRET THAT BIOLOGISTS and wildlife agents never have, and probably never will, see eye to eye on philosophies of wildlife management. The biologist works with population figures that indicate the number of animals that may be harvested and yet maintain healthy breeding stocks. This is accomplished through the establishment of open seasons, bag limits, and restrictions regarding the sex or size of animals that may be harvested. In theory, game herds may be kept in check by cropping, which keeps the proper ratio of females to males to fit the habitat. Adequate food is a key, provided other factors are suitable, and by keeping a close surveillance on supplies, you harvest up or down accordingly. If the population is building too fast you knock it down by killing the females. If it's on the decline you might take males only and try to shift hunting pressure to higher population areas. Stocks should never get so low that seasons have to be closed; sometimes this is an indication of poor management.

Unfortunately, man and nature often refuse to follow the rules, and theories work best in studies or on paper. The enforcement agent knows that in order to accomplish all the proper balances, people must be managed and the bottom line is that people usually cannot, and will not, be managed. The illegal taking of fish and game is big business, and it can throw the best biological plans into a continuous cocked hat. This, coupled with severe winters (Mother Nature's way of keeping animal populations in check) and the political arena with its own theories on wildlife management, provides a nearly impossible situation for managing wildlife populations.

Colleges do not seem to prepare biologists for the real world, and it takes years before most can accept the real facts of life — you don't manage game, but try to manage people instead. Given man's breeding potential, which doesn't have the cyclic checks and balances of animal populations, and his need for land, it can and will eventually lead to the demise of much of the wildlife kingdom that we know today. Aldo Leopold defined conservation as a state of harmony between man and land. Show me any harmony today between the land developer, the environmentalist, the hunter, the fisherman, the geologist, or other users of "the land," and I'll buy the theory that wildlife populations can be managed. The only place this can be accomplished to any degree of success is on refuges and parks, and even those are in doubt.

The administrators of some of our national and state parks refused to believe that well-organized, guided hunts were being conducted within the boundaries of these hallowed sanctuaries until the U.S. Fish and Wildlife Service, using undercover agents, broke up several rings. One agent was taken on a hunt inside Yellowstone National Park for a bighorn sheep. Without causing suspicion, he and his illegal guide even stopped to talk with the park ranger on the drive out with the sheep trophy tucked away in the trunk of the car.

The State of California was equally embarrassed when an undercover hunter took a guided hunt inside one of the Desert Bighorn Sheep preserves. The guide, a well-respected taxidermist and member of the state's bighorn sheep advisory board, had access to all of the biologists' studies on sheep populations. He was even invited to assist with aerial counts to help map population distributions on the different ranges dictated by seasonal shifts.He used all this good biological information to plan clandestine hunts in an area where there was no competition and where he could manipulate the population to his own advantage. There was no lack of hunters willing to pay almost any fee for the opportunity to take the sheep, the most difficult to take of the four American trophy sheep. The guide's overhead was small, and he needed only a few trusted employees to conduct his lucrative business. Advertising was by word of mouth among poachers who included highly respected business people and elected officials. He did most of the guiding himself and used his helpers to drive and move vehicles to the proper locations.

Once taken, the heads were mounted at his taxidermy shop, which kept them under wraps until they adorned the wall of the "sportsmen". The guide's closed network took at least 75 sheep from a small population thought by biologists and wildlife administrators to be safe from hunters. Interestingly, a nationally known taxidermist blew the whistle on this operation because he could not get a piece of the action.

Anyone who believes that animals are not being taken from wildlife sanctuaries today, or any biologist who cannot believe that the illegal gun pressure is upsetting his sacred management philosophies, is due for a rude awakening. Most game departments are made up of 5 to 10 biologists for every enforcement agent. In my opinion, the ratio will have to be reversed if a proper balance of management and protection of wildlife is to be attained.

Recent studies in the Lower 48 indicate that the illegal kill of deer may rival the legal kill in many areas, and that fewer than five percent of fish and game law violations are detected by enforcement officers. Considering the vastness of the state and the amount of area patrolled by each officer, it is likely that only one or two percent — or fewer — of the violations of fish and game regulations are detected in Alaska.

Alaska is now deputizing biologists to increase the force of officers in the field. Unfortunately, most biologists cannot effectively involve themselves in enforcement work because they feel it interferes with true wildlife studies and statistics. Few biologists will check a hunting or fishing license while conducting bag checks or a creel census, believing it will bias the sportsman and keep him from cooperating. I have found just the opposite to be true. Most wildlife users want you to check their license if you make contact because they have purchased the license and want you to know they have complied with the law. I contacted a 70-year-old sports fisherman once, and after checking his license (there were no provisions for senior citizen licenses in Territorial days) he thanked me saying, "I've been buying a license for over 50 years and this is the first time I've ever been checked. It makes me feel that it was worth it after all these years, and I'm proud to show it to you." The individual who doesn't have a license will understandably resent being checked because he knows he has a problem. If he is asked for information about his hunting or fishing success and is not asked for a license, he will have beaten the system, and this may encourage him and his friends to violate fish and game laws.

Any system that attempts to determine the take of wildlife, whether it be by compulsory tagging and reporting, personal interviews, or using formulas on electronic computers, has to add in the fudge factor of the illegal take. This is all guess work, and from what we know about the illicit guides, professional poachers, homesteaders, trappers, or Natives killing game in any number at any season because they think they have a right to, the figure has always been low. This error has jumped up and caught managers in the past and will continued to be a big factor in attempting to provide quantified fish and game limits without damaging breed stocks.

One biologist who I worked with for years seemed to have that uncanny ability of balancing wildlife research, management, enforcement and common sense all together into his work as a game manager. Sig Olson was one of those rare individuals who gained the respect of all who worked with or for him. Being the son of Sigurd Olson, the nationally known wilderness expert and author, must have helped in molding his character, for like his dad, he has genuine concern for people and nature. In addition to being a wildlife expert, he is also a cartoonist, a talent which was put to good use many times to relieve the tension of heated debates during Game Commission meeetings and public hearings. Often during a serious in-house discussion when tempers had a tendency to flare, Sig's mind would go to work and those next to him would see the pencil and pad fly into action. Within a few minutes a humorous caricature dealing with the controversy would start its way around the room. You always knew where the cartoon was because the individual reading it was smiling or in some cases, laughing out loud. On one occasion during a very tense debate a series of muffled laughs crept around the room. Finally, Regional Director Clarence Rhode, who was chairing the meeting as executive director of the Game Commission, threw up his hands and said, "Obviously one of Sig's cartoons is making its way around the room, and this discussion will have to be recessed until everyone has had a chance to see it." The tense feelings that had prevailed were broken and after the laughter subsided the meeting proceeded in a more sedate manner.

Sig and I flew many missions together, mapping out biological information such as caribou migration patterns and game counts. We were also involved in several search and rescue flights. Even though he is not a pilot, he has many thousands of hours in the air and knows a great deal about flying bush Alaska. He traveled with most of us happily doing more than his share of preflight maintenance and putting the planes to bed . for the night. I never heard him complain about getting out and pushing the tail around in deep snow. (Some of his thoughts on being a pusher are mentioned in the chapter on the Gullwing.)

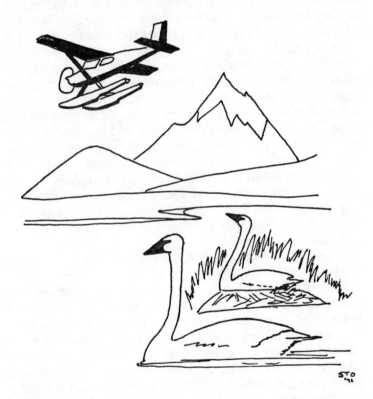

During the tense moments when the weather got bad in the mountains or the engine missed a few beats (in one case failing completely), he remained calm and made the situation lighter with humorous comments. A great guy to have along when the old axiom about flying being "hours and hours of boredom broken up by moments of stark terror" came into play.

We also had our arguments in the cockpit about our position over the ground. This was especially important when mapping out the location of bands of animals and significant observations such as nests of peregrine falcons or the camp of ground crews who were waiting for us to make an air drop of supplies.

If you take a look at a map sometime of that area bounded by the Yukon River on the north, the Canadian border on the east, the Tanana River on the south, and the Steese Highway on the west, you will notice the entanglement of intertwined watersheds going in all directions where the Chena, Salcha and Goodpasture rivers flowing south divide from the Charlie, Forty Mile and Seventy Mile rivers and Birch Creek flowing north. This has to be one of the most confusing pieces of country in Alaska to navigate at low altitude, let alone while trying to pinpoint the location of sightings. It is also the home of the Forty-mile caribou herd, and we spent a good deal of time mapping migration patterns east and west from the calving grounds to the wintering range. Tracking was easy in the winter, and the herd could be located on most trips, however, after the snow was gone the herd was a real challenge to find. These wandering critters leave summer trails that show up as deep brown ruts in valley muskeg. The trails become faint lines as they cross mountain ridges. The trick is to get down low in the valleys to track their travel and then circle the ridge tops to determine which valley they went into next.

The pilot did the tracking, the biologist did the mapping, and together they tried to agree on which way they were going. After circling, climbing and going down into the valleys time after time, you have a tendency to get confused. You think you're in the headwaters of the Charlie River but notice after a while that the stream is running in the wrong direction and you're back on the Salcha or Goodpasture. The only thing you can do when you get completely discombobulated is climb to altitude, check the watersheds, determine your exact position (if possible) and then go back down into the valley again. This was one of the reasons the surveys were only conducted in clear weather. The other, of course, was the need for bright sunshine to outline the shadows of the trails. More than once we became so disoriented and frustrated we had to go to Eagle or Circle and land for a break before continuing.

It was during one of these surveys that Sig and I had a complete disagreement on the location of an obscure peak named West Point on the map. At 5,865 feet it's the highest point in the center of the several watersheds in the area. There are several others between 5,500 to 5,700 feet. In fact, all the hills appear to be about the same height, and you have to be high enough to get a clear picture of all the rivers to be able to identify an individual apex. On this trip Sig, as usual, was drawing our route of flight on the chart in pencil when we lost the caribou tracks. We circled and circled at altitude in all directions, and it wasn't long before the pencil lines were as confused as we were. I pointed out where I thought we were and he emphatically defended the position marked on the map. Since he was the navigator while I had to pay strict attention to the valleys, river bends and box canyons, I had to admit that he had the edge. Finally I pointed to a peak and loudly proclaimed it to be West Point, and he just as emphatically pointed to another and said, "No, that's West Point." The argument lasted for about five minutes with each of us directing the other's attention to matching details on the map with specific river bends and other peaks. We gave up with neither of us convincing the other and ended the debate by declaring that West Point really didn't exist. It was just a figment of someone's imagination run wild while making the map.

Later when we were in the office Sig showed me the map with the supposed track of the plane penciled in and the caribou trails ending in confusion at the head of the Salcha or the Charlie or the Goodpasture rivers or somewhere else. On the point on the map where West Point was indicated, there was a cartoon of the two of us squared off in fisticuffs with the words "biff", "bang", "pow", over the top of the picture.

Another map had fisticuffs marked where the tracks of the plane ended abruptly on an unnamed lake northwest of Fort Yukon. This occurred during the search for Clarence Rhode. The search was into its third week, and Sig and I were teamed up flying out of Fairbanks and Fort Yukon in a Cessna 180 on floats. My wife was staying at Sig's Fairbanks home with his wife Esther while awaiting the birth of our third daughter. We would call headquarters and receive a series of numbered quadrats given by latitude and longitude assigned from the master map which directed us to the area we were to search next. Once over the location, as indicated by our map, we would stay within the boundaries of the deliniated area until we were confident we had covered the entire tract 100 percent. In the mountains this required many hours of flying and at times several days to complete one six-mile square. We usually started at the top of a peak circling downward to its base or where it intersected with another. After the higher altitude work was finished, we flew the valleys and canyons from every angle until we agreed that we had given it our best shot. We were in constant radio contact with headquarters or another aircraft for safety purposes and to provide information on weather and search progress. Once an aircraft finished a series of connecting squares it was assigned another series, and a different plane would move in and search the area all over again. The country was so rugged that we all knew a wrecked plane could be missed during a fleeting glance at the map or aircraft instruments, so the most probable country was checked and rechecked by different crews.

Weather, of course, played a big factor, and there were times when only the valleys could be searched, or with a low overcast, only the mountain tops. If the area we were assigned had serious weather problems, we called headquarters and obtained another. Such was the case on the day of the abruptly ending track on the map. We had been given several areas on the north side of the Brooks Range that were supposed to have searchable weather. This had been verified by the military plane sent up at dawn each day to give a high altitude weather briefing for the entire region. Weather patterns change very rapidly in late fall, however, and this day was no exception. There was a heavy overcast that seemed to be lowering as we headed up the East Chandalar to the Junjik River where there is a low pass through the mountains to the quadrat we had been assigned. In addition to the thickening clouds there was a strong south wind that was funneling through the passes, causing turbulence. As we approached the summit of the pass we were a little apprehensive, because it appeared that the weather was getting worse and we had to make a sharp right turn to get through the valley before we could tell how bad it was on the other side. Once committed we would have to go through because it was too narrow in the canyon to turn around. I tried to slow up for a look at the point of no return. However the strong tail wind and turbulence made it impossible, and before we could say yea or nay we had no choice but to proceed to the other side. Sort of like threading a needle the morning after the night before.

What we saw, or could not see, on the other side of the divide was not very encouraging. It was lousy with snow showers, low visibility and turbulence, so we had to get back on the south side again. One thing we both agreed to was that we did not want to reverse our course through that same pass. The violent ups and downs were not conducive to calm nerves while considering whether or not the wings were going to stay bolted on, so we proceeded east and found a wider valley with less turbulence that took us back to the Junjik River. Once in better weather we again called headquarters and gave them an on-site weather report. We were directed to another search area of heavily timbered country on the Yukon flats. We located the coordinates on our map and proceeded to fly back and forth over the level and boring countryside with little hope of finding anything.

Sig was mapping our progress, wondering how close we were to the lines he drew on the chart since there were few landmarks for guidance. It was like mowing a lawn except we were using compass headings to keep the lines straight instead of the tracks of the mower. Here was another place that the map would be cartooned with "biffs," "bams," and "pows" because we were in disagreement again as to our specific location. Then it happened. The engine malfunctioned, the cabin filled with smoke, and we were faced with an emergency. The engine chose its time to have a problem right over a nice round lake. It was fortunate irony for us because we had been flying over miles of solid forest where there were no lakes and in rugged mountains where there was nothing but rocks beneath us. At 500 feet altitude there wasn't much time to do anything but shut the engine off and land while we could still see. The smoke was thick, and even with both side windows open visibility through the windshield was definitely restricted. The landing was tense but uneventful and when the plane came to rest in the middle of the lake I asked Sig to get out and open up the cowling on his side so we could assess the problem.

I climbed out on the left float and started peering inside the access door. All I could see was oil dripping everywhere, indicating a likely broken oil line spewing lubricating oil blown all over the hot engine. As I was looking for the source of the leak I heard a strange banging noise. I asked Sig if he knew what was causing the banging. He answered, "Man that's my knees shaking against the side of the plane, and I can't get them to stop!" That produced a laugh, and I finally decided that we had to get to shore and remove the cowling. Sig grabbed the paddle that was tied on the float spreader bars and began making like a voyageur, pushing the plane toward the nearest bank. After every 10 or 15 strokes he cupped his hands and yelled "help" at the top of his lungs. This broke a lot of the tension as we both laughed and wondered who beside the two loons at the far end of the lake would hear his plaintive call out here in the middle of nowhere. That didn't bother Sig. He kept yelling anyway.

Once ashore we found that the source of the leaking oil was a ruptured oil cooler. With that knowledge I had Sig string out the radio's trailing antenna, and we had our second piece of luck. We could not contact Fairbanks but we were able to talk loud and clear to our Anchorage aircraft office more than 500 miles away. I apprised them of the problem and within a short time Tom Wardleigh, assistant aircraft supervisor, was enroute to us in a Grumman Goose with a new oil cooler and oil. Search headquarters in Fairbanks were advised, so after removing the cowling and cooler all we could do was sit and wait. We built a fire and boiled up a pot of tea just in time for one of the other Cessna 180's to land and join us. Averill Thayer had heard our message, and since he had been only 60 miles away, he had dropped in to help.

Several hours later Tom arrived with the new parts. He had been unable to locate a gasket, but had some blank gasket material and began tracing out the pattern and cutting one out. With many helping hands working together we had the new cooler on and all the bolts safety wired in a short time. A test run showed everything to be working normally so everyone shook hands and departed on our separate ways. Tom headed for Anchorage, Ave for Fairbanks, and Sig and I for Fort Yukon where we would spend the night before starting out again for our search area on the north side, weather permitting.

After 20 minutes of flying the head and oil temperature gauges started to climb. I was in contact with Tom and mentioned this to him indicating that if they got much higher I would land. There was a long pause in the radio conversation and then he replied, "That gasket is made like a square figure eight and I'll bet we left out the middle section which is allowing the oil to bypass part of the cooler, causing it to overheat. You'll have to take it apart again and check it out!"

The reply from me was, "Thanks. I'll keep you advised. We're landing in a lake about 20 miles northeast of Fort Yukon to let the temperatures cool down." We finally limped into the village late in the evening just before dark. We would wait until morning to again tackle the oil cooler.

The next morning we removed the cooler and determined that the gasket indeed had been cut wrong, so we went to work making another. This was a trial and error process, with many choice words coming forth as we labored on the muddy bank of the Yukon River trying to keep from dropping parts, bolts, and screws in the murky waters. Being a mechanic was not my bag and patience was not my virtue, so the pressure mounted. After attaching the cooler, we again safety wired all the bolts holding it in place. This required threading a long piece of stainless wire through a hole in each bolt head and making necessary twists and turns to keep it from coming loose. My knuckles kept getting barked from scrapes along pieces of metal. All this time Sig was making with the smiles and cheerful remarks as he handed me tools and bolts. At one point as I was about to try a short cut, he stopped me and said, "My grandmother used to say 'Be the job big or small, do it well or not at all.' " This broke the ice and we stopped long enough to have a breather and a chuckle. Before the job was finished that phrase was to be repeated several times and became our theme for the remainder of our time on the search.

Although Sig and I have both been moved around the state on job assignments for several conservation agencies, we are still able to get together once in a while for a canoe trip or to share a campfire. We continue to have the same concerns about Alaska's wildlife and try to compare today's standards of measurement with those that prevailed during the fifties. Our conversations go on long after the campfire has died to a few glowing coals, and although we don't agree on every issue, we can acknowledge that there was a better balance back then between enforcement and management.

Hanging on a wall in my house is a reminder of these good

old days with Sig. It's one of his cartoons showing a pilot working on the engine of an airplane. Nuts and bolts are flying in every direction and the pilot is obviously very frustrated. Underneath is the caption "Be the job big or small, do it well or not at all". Its frame is made from sloppily cut molding fastened together with bent nails. It's one of my most cherished possessions, a reminder of a memorable occasion and a good friend. ■

Chapter 18

Modus Operandi

HISTORICALLY, GAME LAW ENFORCEMENT is the oldest tool of game management, the original goal of which was the preservation of breeding stocks, and the management of harvests. We find the first written game law in the Old Testament. Deuteronomy 22:6 forbade the taking of game in such quantities which would reduce basic breeding stocks (to preserve the dam or hen as breeding stock). Marco Polo wrote of the Great Kublai Khan (1259-1294), who enforced the first system of open and closed seasons on many game animals and birds during their breeding periods. The Magna Carta signed in 1215 recognized the importance of wildlife to the people of England, and it became the legal foundation of the present system of game administration in the United States. In 1646 the Rhode Island town of Portsmouth closed the "deere" hunting season from May until November; any violator was to be fined five pounds. Half the fine went to the person who brought the culprit to court, and the other half to the town's treasury. By the time of the American Revolution, 12 of the 13 colonies had closed seasons and methods and means of taking game.

At the end of the Revolution the Common Law of England was applied and determined that the state (in the same capacity as the King) owns all wildlife within its boundaries, and holds it in trust for the people. Game within a territory acquired by the national governnment after the adoption of the federal constitution became the property of the United States in trust for the benefit of the people of the states subsequently organized out of such territory. Until the organization of such states, the federal government can regulate the taking of game.

Federal laws, then, prevailed in Alaska until statehood was granted. Alaska, as a state, assumed responsibility for its fish and game on January 1, 1960. The federal laws were attempts to give protection to mammals, birds and fish through a series of congressional acts beginning in 1868. A list of those acts are as follows:

1868 — Act of July 22, 1868 (15 Stat. L., 240, 241)
Provided a criminal code for the Territory of Alaska and placed authority to regulate taking of fur animals, land and marine, under the Secretary of the Treasury.

1899 — Act of March 3, 1899 (30 Stat. L., 1253,1279, 1281)
Restatement of above.

1900 — Act of June 6, 1900 (31 Stat. L., 321,322, 323)
Made further provision for a civil government for Alaska.

1902 — Act of June 7, 1902 (32 Stat. L., 327)
Provided for the protection of game in Alaska.

1908 — Act of May 11, 1908 (35 Stat. L., 102)
Amended the act of 1902.

1910 — Act of April 21, 1910 (36 Stat. L., 326, 327)
Provided for management of the seal fisheries of Alaska.

1912 — Act of August 24, 1912 (37 Stat. L., 512)
Created a legislative assembly for the Territory of Alaska, to confer legislative power thereon. This legislation denied territorial authority in game, fish and fur laws.

1920 — Act of May 31, 1920 (41 Stat. L., 694, 715, 716, 717)
Made appropriations for Department of Agriculture and transferred powers and duties with regard to land fur-bearing animals in Alaska to the Secretary of Agriculture.

1924 — Joint Resolution No. 34 (43 Stat. L., 668)
Provided that the powers and duties conferred upon
the Governor of Alaska for the protection of wild
game animals and wild birds in Alaska be
transferred to and be exercised by the Secretary of
Agriculture.

On January 13, 1925, Congress passed the Alaska Game Law,
which superseded all previous federal laws and regulations for
the protection of game animals, land fur animals, and birds in
the territory. This did not include the Migratory Bird Treaty, the
Lacey Act, and laws protecting animals and birds on federal reservations. It authorized the Secretary of Agriculture to make suitable
regulations to accomplish the purpose of the respective laws and
the employment of personnel and equipment to enforce the acts
and regulations. This function was transferred to the Secretary
of Interior with the creation of the Fish and Wildlife Service in
1940.

Alaska wardens, later known as Alaska enforcement agents,
enforced provisions of the Alaska game laws and regulations,
federal wildlife and commercial fisheries laws, as well as territorial
acts in Alaska and on the high seas. The small staff of agents
was supplemented with the use of deputies, temporary patrolmen,
and stream guards during the busy seasons.

Before 1925, moose, sheep, and caribou were legally killed
and sold on the market or to supply meat to road crews,
roadhouses, and dog teams. This became illegal under Alaska
game law. It took years of hard enforcement to stop the wanton
slaughter of game animals for profit by market hunters.
Strychnine poison was commonly used in the early days of
trapping for the taking of furbearers and required an intense effort
on the part of the "fur wardens" to eliminate the practice.

The first wardens patrolled their districts by boat, snowshoes,
and dog teams. Their's was a lonesome and, at times, an
unrewarding life. They were enforcing game regulations that had
little support with bush residents, most of whom were dependent
on wild meat, fish or furs for subsistence. Hunters who once sold
meat on the open market in Fairbanks and other towns became
outlaws when they bartered or sold parts of game animals to
others. Trappers who once carried cans of poison instead of the
heavy steel traps were arrested and fined. Dog team drivers who
hauled freight and mail and depended on moose and caribou

as dog feed had to find another source of food for their teams. (The sale of dried salmon became big business in the river towns.) Logging and mining camps that used wild meat in the mess halls had to ship in domestic beef. Additionally, there were seasons and bag limits to be concerned with.

Old reports that were in the files when I transferred to McGrath in 1956 gave real insight into what Game Warden Wayne House, one of my predecessors, and other wardens were up against. Catching bush-savvy people with illegal goods was extremely difficult, to say the least. Everyone knew what direction the game warden was headed in when he left headquarters, and the word went out by "moccasin telegraph," which some said was faster than a speeding bullet. Knowing this, the warden often doubled back to head out in another direction. His hope was to arrive at a particular poacher's place of business before the warning word got out.

If and when the warden was able to catch a poacher with the goods, he faced another monumental task — prosecuting the person in court and obtaining a conviction. The word got out not long after a few cases were tried that the best way to beat the system was to demand a jury trial. This way a defendent could go before a jury of his neighbors (or people living the same lifestyle), and as long as he wasn't an outcast, he would probably receive a not-guilty verdict. Each member of the jury probably thought, "There but for the grace of God go I . . . and next time it might be me!"

There was a case report in the file about "Highpower Swede," which interested me because the man was living in a cabin upriver from McGrath. He came to town regularly to sell loads of wood and to pick up supplies. His gas-powered scow flew an American flag above the stern, and his wife, a local Indian woman, stood in the bow ready to help beach and unload the four-foot-long cord wood. I enjoyed their visits and the stories he told in thick Swedish accent of the early days. Early on in our talks I asked him about his nickname of the "Highpower Swede," since most of the monikers given were the result of an interesting occurence or particular trait.

In his case it was attributed to a difference of opinion between him and his brother, both of whom had trekked from Sweden to Alaska during the early 1900s. Both were stubborn and each had a very definite conception on what type of rifle was the best for killing game. The brother was an advocate of older rifles with low muzzle velocity. He claimed they wasted less meat when an animal was killed. Highpower, on the other hand, went in for the newer calibers that were being developed, figuring that they anchored the larger game in their tracks when shot and what meat was wasted was compensated by fewer animals wounded or lost. The argument went on through the years, and those who got involved ended up naming the brothers the "Lowpower" and the "Highpower" Swedes. It was probably a lot easier than trying to pronounce their tongue twisting names anyway.

The case report on Highpower was written by Wayne House. He had apprehended Highpower on the Northfork of the Kuskokwim River with a boat containing three moose. The regulation stated that a person could have only one moose in his possession at any one time, and the season was prescribed as September 1 through December 31. A total of five moose could be taken by a resident and two by a nonresident. Being an alien he was allowed to take two moose with only one in possession at any one time. Highpower was caught over the bag limit and over the possession limit — caught but not convicted. He requested a jury trial in McGrath. Six men tried and true were chosen as jurors, and the trial took place in the local meeting hall (probably one of the bars). Warden Wayne House presented his case, which was taken from his written report on the events of the day he apprehended Highpower. He gave an exact count of the number of pieces of meat in the boat and indicated that 12 moose legs added up to three freshly killed moose. Next it was Highpower's turn to tell his side of the story. No doubt he looked back and forth from the U.S. commissioner to the jury before making a brief statement on where he went hunting, how he needed the meat to survive the winter, and could he help it if his moose had 12 legs? That was his total defense, and the jury of his peers found him not guilty.

When I asked Highpower about the circumstances of the case he just shrugged and said, "Yar, shure, that was funny looking moose — 12 legs."

There were still a few of the old wardens around when I first went to work for the Fish and Wildlife Service. Sam White, the world's first flying warden, was a great source of information, and we developed a long-lasting friendship over the years I was in Fairbanks. He came to Alaska from Maine where he had worked as a lumberjack. After a few years of traveling around the territory doing odd jobs he went to work as a game protector in 1927. With his background as a woodsman and believing in wildlife conservation, he felt he was qualified to take on Alaska's poachers. Looking back at his career he said he had the satisfaction of putting out of business several of the hard-core poachers who continued to indiscriminately use poison on wildlife and slaughtered big game for individual profit. At the same time he was able to look the other way when those in need took an occasional animal out of season. Like so many of his colleagues, he found out that the poachers were not the biggest problem — it was the administrators dictating unrealistic policies from Juneau and Washington, D.C.

He did his patrolling with a dog team, boat, snowshoes and motorcycle. The motorcycle was used in Fairbanks and on the limited road system. When running errands around town he tied his dogsled behind the two-wheel vehicle to haul groceries and freight.

His big goal was to promote the use of an airplane to more effectively patrol his vast area of responsibility. All his pleas and memos fell on deaf ears, however, since his superiors failed to envision the aircraft as an enforcement and management tool. In desperation he finally bought his own plane, a Bone Golden Eagle monoplane, and started using it at no cost to the government in a last effort to promote its use.

Every spring one of his assignments was counting the moose in the Blair Lakes district south of Fairbanks using his dog team and snowshoes. This area, which encompassed approximately one hundred square miles, had a high density of animals and was used as a barometer to gauge the winter survival rate. The year he bought his aircraft he used it for the spring count and made the first aerial census of moose in Alaska. He proudly submitted his report of what he felt was the most reliable tally ever accomplished in the territory. For his efforts he received a terse and nasty memo from the regional administrator telling him they would not accept his report as accurate and to go back out and count the moose on foot like he was supposed to.

He continued using his plane to patrol his northern district at no cost to the government and proved its worth on many occasions. Grudgingly the bureaucrats acknowledged the merits of his efforts, but Sam felt little credibility in this new shift in position and finally resigned his position in disgust. Not long afterward the service bought a few aircraft and put them to use, finally realizing how effective they really were as patrol vehicles. Years later Sam was finally credited for his efforts but by then he was bitter and felt little pleasure in the back pats he received.

Sam started his own flying business and became well known as a bush pilot. He eventually went to work for Wien Airlines, and when he was in his seventies he was still flying a Cessna 180 on the Huslia-Hughes-Bettles run. It was about that time that Wien required their bush pilots to have an instrument rating. This would have required a considerable amount of studying and 40 hours of flight training, so Sam decided it was time to hang up his goggles and retire. When people asked him why he quit flying, he would chuckle and tell them it was due to the lack of a formal education.

With the advent of the airplane the entire enforcement program changed direction. The wardens popped into the most remote areas of Alaska unannounced, making it difficult for the hard-core poachers to continue their activities without the fear of being arrested. This was especially true in winter when trails and tracks in the snow were like roadmaps of a person's activities. Wardens became proficient at tracking from the aircraft, and once they were able to determine how an individual was conducting his illegal activities, they dropped off additional men with snowshoes and packs at strategic locations. These hardy troopers would walk out the trails, gather the evidence, and eventually arrest the offender. It was a whole new way of doing business, and the results were rewarding. Also, attitudes among the populace were changing. The majority condoned the taking of game by the bush dwellers regardless of regulatory seasons as long as it was needed. They started supporting the law banning the sale of wildlife for personal gain and the use of poison. It was a slow process, but little by little conservation laws were recognized as necessary and the tide started turning in favor of the enforcers. Most wardens were not hard-nosed individuals, and they realized they needed the support of the people in their uphill fight to regulate the harvest as the population boom of the forties started. They turned their backs on minor infractions and avoided confrontations with the locals on traditional taking as long as it was within the bounds of a needed food source.

Sam White told how he handled one of the traditional illegal practices in Fairbanks. Every spring it was customary to hunt a few of the incoming ducks and geese which were found on the open sloughs and ponds around town. This was not a major problem in the 1930s since the take by Alaskans was limited and made a very minor dent into the nesting population. Still,

the Migratory Bird Treaty Act said the hunting season was closed between March 10 and September 1, so the taking was an infraction of the federal law, and the warden had his duty to uphold if he observed anyone in the act of hunting. Sam took care of this by announcing in the local newspaper when he was leaving town and how long he would be gone. This was the signal that allowed a few days of harvesting, and the ritual was observed without problem for several years. Finally, as Fairbanks grew, the practice had to be stopped. It came to a head for Sam when he returned to Fairbanks and found out that a few hunters had built a blind on the edge of Weeks Field, the local airport. Some of the pilots had complained about the shooting, and the last straw was when he went to his hangar and found that some of his airplane parts had been used for constructing the blind.

The large influx of people to the North during and after World War II prompted an increase in the number of wildlife enforcement agents and a crackdown on all infractions of the law. Clarence Rhode became regional director in 1947 and made a big push for airplanes. Being a pilot himself he saw the need for a force of agents equipped with aircraft to effectively patrol Alaska. He manipulated the transfer of surplus equipment and parts from the military, and for once the Service had the mobility it needed to get around.

It was at this time that the U.S. Fish and Wildlife Service grew out of its infancy into the beginning of a large complex conservation organization. Biologists were hired and studies were initiated to learn the intricate patterns of animal and fish populations, migration patterns of waterfowl, and breeding potential of wildlife in the far northern environments to effectively manage the game resources. Commercial fishing was big business with a large division to handle the laws and problems of the industry. A predator division was added when it was shown that a balance was needed between wolves, moose, and caribou if the hunting stocks were going to be increased.

When I went to work there were approximately 25 enforcement agents in the Alaska region. Four of us were at Fairbanks. We had two aircraft for patrolling the northern half of the territory, a Piper Pacer and a Gullwing Stinson. Each of us had a Chevrolet Suburban patrol vehicle (Ray Woolford, the chief, had a sedan), and we had a riverboat. There was no shortage of snowshoes, and we could get those replaced any time we wore out a pair. Usually they were broken in transportation or when we used them under an airplane ski to get it turned around on slick snow or ice.

We traveled constantly and were effective because nobody knew where we were going to show up next. Jim King and I were bachelors in 1953 and 1954 and we seldom took a day off, working in excess of 80 hours a week most of the time. We altered our patrols as the seasons dictated and tried to maintain a visible profile knowing our efforts were token at best. We were pleasant and amiable with sportsmen in the pursuit of legal hunting and fishing enjoyment but were hard-nosed and calloused with poachers that took illegal wildlife for personal gain.

One avid sportsfisherman is probably still telling his friends that the game wardens were everywhere and that there was just no way to violate the game laws in Alaska. This individual was an army officer who was transferred to Fairbanks in the spring of 1954. He went on his first fishing trip in April to Fielding Lake with a small group of military friends. The ice on the lake was still solid, allowing those willing to walk a mile or more access to excellent grayling fishing in the inlet streams that were open and running. There were abut 10 fishermen there that Sunday when Jim and I walked in to check licenses and bag limits. The officer engaged us in a conversation about fishing and hunting, indicating he was going to be stationed here for two years and planned to get out on every day he had off. We briefed him on the laws and regulations and wished him luck. Three weeks later we launched the riverboat for the first trip up the Chena River. About 10 miles upstream we checked a boat with several men enjoying a day of fishing and relaxation. One turned out to be the army captain we had checked at Fielding Lake. "Boy," he said, "you guys sure get around," after we advised him we knew he had a license and would not have to dig it out. We acknowledged the fact that we tried to cover as much of the district as possible and said our goodbye and goodluck. When we returned home we remarked that the contact with the captain was an interesting coincidence.

That summer Jim and I were involved in weekend aircraft patrols of the Yukon River from Kaltag to the Canadian border. For the first time in history fishing on the river was regulated with a complete closure for the taking of salmon during a 48-hour period on weekends. This was an attempt to allow an undisturbed escapement of the fish on the entire Yukon River watershed. The McGrath agents covered the lower river from the mouth to Kaltag. We had previously held meetings in all the villages to advise the people of the new regulation and to advise them that their fishwheels would have to be stopped and nets brought out of the water during the closure. Few were happy about the restriction but they would comply. As a follow-up we flew the river in alternate directions each weekend to make sure everyone observed the restriction. With few exceptions everyone cooperated and we had only one or two infractions.

On one particular hot Saturday we took a detour up to Old John Lake, about 100 miles north of Fort Yukon. This large crystal-clear lake produced excellent lake trout and grayling fishing, and a few of the air taxi opeators out of Fairbanks were beginning to take sports fishermen up there. We spotted a camp on the sandy beach by the inlet, and so we landed to talk with the three men who were fishing. Much to our surprise one of the fishermen turned out to be the army captain again. He threw up his hands, shook his head in disbelief and stated in a loud voice, "I give up, there's no way anyone could ever break the game laws in Alaska." While we were just as amazed at this meeting as he was, we were very professional and agreed that we had a very tight reign on all of Alaska and few violators were able to escape our efforts.

Back in the airplane we looked at one another and wondered how, with a population of over 40,000 people in Fairbanks, could we ever expect to check one sportsman three times over an area of hundreds of square miles in a period of only three months. It had never happened before and it never happened again, but to this day I'm sure he believes we were the most efficient game wardens in the entire United States, and it occurred in Alaska the most remote area under the flag.■

Chapter 19

The Spoilers

THE ENFORCEMENT DIVISION OF THE U.S. Fish and Wildlife Service enforced the provisions of Alaska game law, which gave protection to all game animals, birds, and fish. Emphasis was placed on intensive patrols during hunting and trapping seasons, investigating violations and prosecuting violators through the Federal Court systems. During the off seasons, patrol efforts were conducted to limit the illegal kill of wildlife by individuals for personal gain or because of inherent desires to eliminate predators interfering with a harvest of game or fish for profit, i.e., most commercial fishermen developed a dislike for brown bear, that they felt competed for the valuable salmon stocks and many hunted these valuable carnivores with a vengeance, killing every one on sight.

As sport hunting of big game became more popular, aided by more advanced mobile equipment for reaching all parts of Alaska, enforcement agents had to be trained as investigators to be effective in coping with a new breed of hunter and guide. The guiding industry began to flourish, and many guides were willing to conduct quick hunts using any means to get a trophy for a person willing to pay the substantial fee. Since shipping illegally taken game from the territory was in violation of the Lacey Act, agents were required to conduct investigations involving wildlife shipped to other states and countries. As more pressure was applied through enforcement efforts, the value of trophies increased, and the guides became more efficient in their methods of operation.

At the time of statehood, the U.S. Fish and Wildlife Service was hiring additional agents and requesting Congress to update the game law to put more teeth into its penalty section. With the Statehood Act, the newly created Alaska Department of Fish and Game developed a state fish and wildlife protection division to administer all laws protecting indigenous wildlife. This reduced the federal agent force in Alaska and the emphasis changed from one of patrol warden to patrol investigator, involving intensive investigations of shipment of wildlife taken in violation of state laws. Time was afforded to visiting the Native villages, explaining the provisions of the Migratory Bird Treaty Act and initiating an enforcement program in the progressive areas. This was met with armed resistance by three Bethel residents who shot at my aircraft with shotguns and rifles as I circled their blind. They succeeded in hitting the side of the plane with bird shot without doing much damage, and fortunately missed with the rifle shots. They then proceeded to shoot at two of our agents, Jim Branson and Mil Zahn, who had landed on the river ice and were proceeding toward the blind on foot. Again their shots were not true, and when they observed Jim and Mil continuing their efforts to make contact with my help in the airplane, they took off leaving behind two dog teams, all their gear, and the illegally taken wildlife. They were subsequently arrested and later convicted of armed assault.

Back in Washington, D.C., Senator Gruening improperly determined that the treaty did not apply to the Natives and completely confused the issue, causing the stir which is still being felt today. As a result, the controversy is still in a state of limbo to the detriment of several valuable species of waterfowl which may be in danger due to the illegal taking of birds and eggs in the spring.

In 1974 the enforcement division was reorganized again and our titles were changed to that of "special agents." We became more involved with complicated investigations. Wildlife was and still is big business, and guides, taxidermists, outfitters and importers organized into a multi-million dollar industry. It was necessary to infiltrate the illicit dealers with undercover agents and funds. As the Special Agent in Charge of Alaska I set up the first of these operations in Alaska. We were able to get two of our agents posing as hunters-clients on an illegal polar bear hunt. The results were rewarding since the guides were linked with a big taxidermy firm in Seattle known to be dealing in unlawful hides and furs. The case reached out to illegal hunts in Montana and California and opened up everyone's eyes as to how big the business was. Unfortunately the results in court were less rewarding because we were dealing with misdemeanor crimes, and the district courts were not in harmony with our efforts. Our labors weren't in vain, however. Our success encouraged the state legislature to fund Alaska protection officers conducting several outstanding undercover operations which were prosecuted with excellent results. Planes were confiscated and substantial fines were levied. Jail time was served by several well-known guides. The work has continued, and not too surprisingly, some of the same guides have been caught repeatedly. Greed knows no bounds and as long as there is a person willing to pay for an illegal hunt there will be a guide willing to risk all to accommodate him. The big question to non-hunters is why? Why spend thousands of dollars to get an illegal animal and risk heavy fines, jail, the loss of the trophy, and the possibility of being ostracized by peers? The answer has to be ego. These are not hunters; they are killers after a quick and easy entry in a record book.

A good example of how far a person with means will go to get in a record book occurred in Alaska several years back. A nationally known "sportsman" with many recorded kills to his credit was also a board member for a museum of natural history in one of the southwestern states. The directors of this museum requested and were granted from the Fish and Wildlife Service a permit to obtain a musk-ox bull from the Nunivak Island Refuge. This was to be made into a full mount for a habitat group that would include a cow and calf to be collected at a later time when funds were available. A permit was issued with the stipulation that the animal would be collected by the refuge manager, much to the consternation of the sportsman-board member. He requested and was granted permission to accompany the biologist in order to oversee the preparation and shipment of the hide, skull and leg bones. However, prolonged bad weather and a tight schedule prompted him to leave Nunivak Island before a large bull could be killed. Later when the animal was taken by the biologist, it was prepared in accordance with instructions from the museum and shipped to New Mexico. Imagine everyone's surprise when the next edition of the Boone and Crockett record book listed this musk-ox as *taken* by the famous hunter. If that were not enough, the hide had been reduced to a cape and made into a head mount that adorned his trophy room. We advised the Boone and Crockett authorities, and they retracted the record. The head was seized and confiscated by our agents. An isolated case you say? Not so, and Fish and Wildlife Service records have many examples of the extremes people will go to to be listed in the "book."

When Theodore Roosevelt and his colleagues formed the Boone and Crockett Club in 1887 they envisioned an organization that would foster sportsmanlike methods of hunting. They encouraged the hunting of big game as a sport for vigorous and masterful people pursuing wildlife by foot, horseback, canoe or dogsled. The "Credo of Fair Chase," was developed to stop the wanton killing of helpless animals such as those caught in traps or deep snow. In 1963 the club added to the fair chase code rules against spotting or herding game from the air. Other rules precluded pursuing game from a motor-powered vehicle.

Since most authorities, including the board members of Boone and Crockett, agree that sportsmanship cannot be legislated, maybe it's time to close the book. Certainly now there are enough records by which hunters can gauge their trophies. There is no need to continue recognizing hero hunters.

Unfortunately, too many organizations foster the kill image, and they too should rewrite their bylaws to end "head hunting." Surely, we can all improve the image of hunting and bring back the nuts and bolts of fair chase. The bandit guide and his combustion engine would fade out of the picture without these people. He would be forced to conduct a "hunt" instead of a "thrill kill." Poor hunting practices must stop sometime, either voluntarily or by mandate, or all hunting will be legislated out of existence. The choice is ours and we had better make it soon.

Our rural neighbors and bush relatives are not so clean either. Where once hunting was a necessary way of life, it has now become a lifestyle. The subsistence issue in Alaska has divided residents into hostile groups, each claiming certain "rights" to the wildlife resources. This battle is being fought in the courts, both state and federal, by fish and game boards, the Department of Fish and Game, the U.S. Fish and Wildlife Service, national parks and other resource agencies. Although many claim it is not a Native versus whites issue, it certainly has divided many from each culture. It appears this issue will be in the courts with appeals and counter appeals for many years.

I attended one of the first subsistence conferences in 1974 as a panel member representing the Fish and Wildlife Service. After listening to several presentations the first day I rewrote the paper I was supposed to give with my own concerns. Interestingly we are no further ahead now than we were then, and in fact, I believe because of recent legislation we have regressed. Here is what I said that day:

> Senator Sackett has very adequately outlined the problems and some very equitable solutions. I agree with many of his thoughts and appreciate his concern; however, I have some ideas as a result of my experiences which I would like to share with you today. Hopefully, they will be taken in the right context from one who has a great respect for the Native people and their cultures.
>
> I believe I am entitled to state a few of my thoughts from both the standpoint of a department representative — specifically a wildlife enforcement agent — and also a former subsistence user.
>
> First of all I came to Alaska seeking a lifestyle and lived within that lifestyle as a trapper for several years — this made me a subsistence user. What was my right to that lifestyle? Certainly I was not a Native Alaskan; however, I trapped and hunted in an area not being used by anyone else. In fact, I bought the line from the trapper that cut many of the trails and built some of the cabins. I hunted and trapped with a boat and a dog team and never was I challenged to my right to use the land for that purpose, nor did I abuse that privilege, and here I use the word privilege because that's really what it was: An American citizen allowed to seek a lifestyle.
>
> Later I accepted a job with the U.S. Fish and Wildlife Service as an enforcement agent trainee because I believed it would allow me to continue being among those people living the same type of lifestyle I enjoyed and at the same time work with an agency I believed was aimed at assuring that all the people had an equal share of the wildlife; at the same time giving needed protection to that resource.
>
> During my early years as an enforcement agent I met many of the old-timers in my travels. I listened with great

interest to their stories about themselves and others they knew and learned that they too came to Alaska seeking a lifestyle much the same as I did. Interestingly, the names of these men have a real meaning here today. Sommer, Vernetti, Huntington, Sackett, Carter and others. These men all married into Native cultures — the same as I did — and many of their children are today's leaders, as I hope some-day mine will be. They were privileged to live that lifestyle, and those that I talked with agreed that as the country was changing, the fur wardens, as we were called, were necessary as referees to assure everybody had that equal chance.

Another distinction sets me aside from everyone in this room. I was shot at for attempting to enforce a treaty law enacted to protect migratory birds during the nesting season. At no time to my knowledge has a Native been arrested for taking migratory birds while truly living by subsistence. Interestingly, the three Natives who shot at me claimed later that they needed the birds to avoid "starving to death." No matter that in their blind, along with the dead ducks, were such high-priced items as liquor, canned meats, and canned strawberry jam, as well as expensive shotguns, .22 rifles, and ammunition.

After many hours of listening to all these presentations I ask the question: What culture or lifestyle are you trying to save? The old spear-harpoon, canoe-kayak true sub-sistence type user or the new highpower, snowmachine, down clothing, electricity, radio, TV lifestyle added to by subsistence hunting and fishing, much the same as some of the rest of Alaskans are living today.

I'm saying that you can't have the best of two worlds, because when you accept the 20th century lifestyle, you must accept the responsibilities it requires.

You can't hunt and fish anytime you want anymore because your numbers are increasing, and the land will not support enough wildlife to provide all you desire.

You Native leaders must teach your young people that they can't be seasonally or permanently employed in urban Alaska and then go to rural Alaska to be a subsistence user for short periods of time. They can't have the best of two worlds. They are either true subsistence users, or they are

incidental takers who must conform to laws and regula-
tions that are necessary to allow all citizens an opportunity
to hunt wildlife while not threatening its existence.

I submit that together we will assure that those with
actual needs will be allowed to take enough wildlife to fill
those needs. At the same time we must educate the inciden-
tal or lifestyle user of his responsibilities. As U.S. citizens
my children are entitled to the same rights as yours. You
and I share the same privileges and responsibilities, and
somewhere there must be a balance.

I was involved in the original Alaska "duck wars," as they have
been called. This story may be written more fully someday, but
briefly, we were advised to enforce the provisions of the Migratory
Bird Treaty Act in the progressive Native villages. This congressional act, which has its authority from a treaty between the

United States, Britain and Mexico, sets a closed season from
March 10 and September 1 for taking migratory waterfowl.
Eskimos and Indians have taken ducks and geese since time
immemorial. They arrived on the nesting grounds, collected eggs
in the early summer and gathered thousands of birds in traps
when they moulted and became flightless. This was not a
problem when the chase was with primitive weapons and later
after firearms were first introduced. As the populations of the

villages exploded, however, the ever-increasing number of hunters with snowmachines, aircraft and outboard motors made significant inroads into important waterfowl populations.

In 1960 and 1961 we made an attempt to lessen the kill rate in the Yukon Delta and along Alaska's coast. We were met with armed resistance and flagrant demonstrations by Natives bringing in illegal birds and demanding to be arrested. They were difficult times, but we followed through and made progress, at least until the politicians intervened. The issue became emotional and one Alaska senator told the Natives it was permissible to take the birds and that he would go to jail with them if the U.S. attorney prosecuted. It went from bad to worse over the years, and to this day the problem is still not solved. There are bureaucrats who believe that by ignoring the problem it will solve itself. Attempts have been made to amend the treaty but to no avail because of the complexities of treaty negotiations. A new treaty with Russia makes provisions for indigents of Alaska to take certain waterfowl in the spring for subsistence. This, however, conflicts with Alaska state law and does not seem to be a good option. Meanwhile, the slaughter increases each spring, and the populations of Pacific black brant and cackling geese that nest almost exclusively in the delta country are taking a nosedive. Studies show large voids where nesting areas have been — voids that increase almost in step with the population growth of nearby villages.

Where will it all end? Maybe the thing to do is let it run its course, and as each species is eliminated, we can record it for posterity just as we did the passenger pigeon, and the great auk. This is facetious, but after years of losing ground more than one game protector has hung up his badge wondering what he really accomplished for the wildlife resource during his career. As one warden put it, "We should just forget about protecting the game. Once it's gone we won't have to worry about it anymore."

We all knew Alaska would change someday, but those of us who loved the country for itself were not prepared for the onslaught that began with the discovery of oil. I know now how the mountain man felt when "his" country was invaded by the homesteaders or how the Indian felt as he watched the white man destroy the buffalo. I wonder at times how well we learned our lesson. A new manifest destiny has taken over this country called the Great Land. One has to only look at the Anchorage skyline to be convinced. Much of the land is going into private ownership, and the no trespassing signs are appearing. A great fight is looming over ownership of navigable rivers.

When we flew around the country in the early fifties it was a thrill to land the floatplane on a newly discovered lake and wonder if we were the first to throw a fishing lure into the water. You don't have to ask the question any more because there is usually a beer can lying along the lake shore that tells it all. I stopped in at Old John Lake a few years ago with a group of law enforcement officials returning from a meeting at Inuvik. The once pristine lake shore where we fished years back was littered with garbage, oil cans and beer cans.

The Alaska game warden today is a mixture of the old and the new. He is unionized and is plagued by rules that dictate his effectiveness. Unless overtime funds are available, he can only work 37½ hours a week. Some have businesses on the side while others are dedicated and spend longer hours on the job in spite of union rules. In 1972 the Fish and Wildlife Protection Division was moved from the Department of Fish and Game to the Department of Public Safety where it is administered under the same operating procedures as the Alaska State Troopers. This was a highly controversial, political move that resulted in better law enforcement procedures, but while the men are better police officers, they understand less about conservation theories because they no longer work with the wildlife managers. There now exists a large breach between biologists and law enforcement agents. So we now have officers enforcing laws without understanding the reasons for their existence, and we have managers requesting regulations that are often unenforceable.

Fortunately I see some bright young people with fresh ideas and common sense for balancing the environmental wildlife and enforcement issues. They will have to walk a delicate tightrope if hunting and fishing are to remain a part of our heritage. It's time for me to move and let someone else take over, but remember, I'm not ready to hang up my rifle and fishing rod yet, so please allow me to pursue my pleasures without the need of an attorney to follow me around, assuring me I am not going afoul of the law. ∎